Defence Offsets Unscrambled

Attention Authors

Manas Publications is fighting a war to tell the world that India can win the battle not only by the bullet but also by pen. We are converting fighters into writers. There is no dearth of intellectuals in our country, however, their knowledge is confined to them only. No sincere effort has been made by any other publisher to channelise their knowledge, that is why the talent of every intellectual remains latent. An author always presents the raw material in the shape of a manuscript and it is the job of the publisher to convert it into a finished product. Manas has been continually motivating intellectuals and publishing their manuscripts for more than three decades and would like to publish your manuscript too. If you or your colleagues have a manuscript ready for publication or are working on it, contact us with a detailed synopsis and list of contents. Manas can also suggest you a suitable title for writing related to your area of expertise. Manas is known for its publishing quality. We take utmost care in publishing and give wide publicity to the book and its author through our national and international distribution network.

Defence Offsets Unscrambled

Gp Capt Sanjiv Aggarwal
Indian Air Force

Manas Publications
(We Convert Fighters into Writers)
New Delhi-110002 (INDIA)

MANAS PUBLICATIONS
(Publishers, Distributors, Importers & Exporters)
4402/5-A, Ansari Road (Opp. HDFC Bank)
Darya Ganj, New Delhi-110 002 (INDIA)
Off. © 23260783, 23265523, Res. © 23842660
Fax: 011-23272766
E-mail: manaspublications@vsnl.com
manaspublications@yahoo.com
Website: www.manaspublications.in

ISBN 978-81-7049-392-1
Rs. 595/-

Typeset at
Manas Publications

Printed in India at
IYN Graphics, Delhi
and published by Mrs Suman Lata for
Manas Publications, 4402/5-A, Ansari Road
(Opp. HDFC Bank),
Darya Ganj, New Delhi-110 002 (INDIA)

CONTENTS

ACKNOWLEDGEMENTS

My sincere and heart-felt thanks to

Laxman Kumar Behera, Research Fellow IDSA

for his intellectual support.

My wife Nita for her support and tolerance.

Our children Dipti and Sameer who, though no longer share the same roof with us, shower us with their enthusiasm and love.

FOREWORD

It has always been a long cherished goal of our nation to have complete self reliance in the Defence sector. Application of "OFFSETS" against capital acquisitions in Defence is a definitive and progressive step towards attainment of this goal.

The offset policy was first articulated in the Defence Procurement Procedure (DPP) in the year 2005. As a natural process of evolvement, this policy has undergone many changes since then to enable it to deliver what was intended at the time it was conceived.

Success of this endeavour and initiative of the Government of India depends on two factors. Firstly, to foreign suppliers' willingness in passing the genuinely required technology as a quid pro quo to the business being given to them. It rests equally on the ability of the Indian Emerging Industry to be able to absorb and adopt such technology and use it effectively.

Given the speciality of Indian bureaucratic overkill to frame rules which can only be interpreted by them in a given situation, a simplistic and orderly rendition of this policy, narrated in a sequential manner for it to be understood by an average person, was necessary. This book is a timely intervention to give all the stakeholders this opportunity.

The author has served the Indian Air Force for 32 years in the Logistics branch dealing primarily with procurements.

He has, therefore, the requisite qualification and the insight to produce a book which I am sure will be of immense value for all the stakeholders. Be it the foreign supplier, the Indian Industry or even us sitting at service headquarters engaged in the business of procurement/spending money.

Air Marshal J Neri
AVSM, VSM
Air Officer-in-Charge Maintenance

PREFACE

Offset, from the point of view of the buyer, is seen as compensation that a buyer seeks from the seller for the purchase of goods or services. Viewing it from the seller's perspective it can be defined as the benefits provided by the contractor to foreign governments as inducements to purchase military goods and services. As these are two opposite and divergent sides of the same coin, so are the two extremely divergent stand points taken by the pro and anti group of people on the efficacy of offset in primarily bringing in high end technology in the country towards greater self sufficiency and indigenization.

The Ayes cite its positive effect on the Indian industry, in terms of growth through rapid industrialisation and in terms of ushering of advanced technology hitherto being denied, the defence industry thus becoming part and parcel of the global supply chain. At the other end of the spectrum the critiques, the Nays, view this as a mere tool being dished out to defence contractors to increase the price without bringing in any significant benefit for the purchasing country. India today represents the largest defence market outside the first world. With a robust growing economy and its growing geo-political role and ambitions, the arm spending is rapidly increasing. The anxiety to spend immediately stems from the profile of the equipment held with its armed forces which shows that more than 50% to be already in obsolescent category and other 35% rapidly moving towards the same category.

Post liberalization, India has transformed into a land of opportunities. This is even true in specific sectors like defence. Upgradation, maintenance and servicing of one of the largest defence forces apart from mammoth purchase orders make a compelling proposition.

Yet, India is also a minefield as the plethora of regulations, regulators, preventive and pre-emptive legislations prove impediments to the non-conversant. These become almost insurmountable barriers given the complexity of the bureaucratic mechanisms, the singular banking and financial norms and the cultural disparateness that pervades.

As the Indian government insists on a quid pro quo in defence contracts, the Offset industry is set to boom. The government of India is building in clauses for international suppliers with an inherent obligation to help further the technology, manufacturing and research and development base in India for the Defence sector. International suppliers are expected to enter into ToT (Transfer of Technology) and manufacturing arrangements in India with specific objective of reducing the risk of future sanction regimes, and the dependency of supply, as well as to motivate the development of an increasingly sophisticated Defence technology and equipment industry inside the country.

India ranks among the top ten countries in the world in terms of military expenditure. The introduction of obligatory offsets against defence contracts and the recent changes in DPP introducing banking credits and introduction of the new category "Buy and Make Indian" are nothing but initiatives by a willing government to attract infusion of FDI in defence related industry. However, India is obviously not an interesting destination for investment yet. The recent initiatives have failed to solicit any buyer. Therefore, unless the basic issues are addressed, these peripheral ramblings are not going to make the industry sit up and take notice. The vendors feel that in case of specially transfer of technology, the returns likely to be generated in view of the FDI cap and lack of controls that they will have due to their minority status, investments are highly unattractive. Investors also want to shift their manufacturing base to India because of the inherent advantages they see in terms of availability of huge technical manpower, established software and design industry, cheap labour, huge home market and at least 30% cheaper manufacturing cost, provided cap is removed and further reforms are ushered in.

With the process of globalization and competitiveness becoming the norm, the Indian Defence industry has to rise to the needs of the hour in creating collaborative partnerships in tandem with the global and Indian partners. This will create an atmosphere to promote indigenous manufacture of defence equipment and help India emerge as global hub for defence manufacturing. This will also open a sea of opportunity for the entrepreneurs for establishing SMEs in niche fields where India excels and become a part of the global environment. With 40000 crores worth offset on the anvil, everybody wants to take a holy dip in this "kumbh" mela! It is "Nirvana".

This book is nothing but a dedication to the emerging defence industry in the country and is a small effort to make all the stakeholders understand the processes and the nitty gritty of the Byzantine, opaque and immature regulatory and acquisition structure in a simple and sequential manner.

Efforts have been made to make available all possible information concerning the offsets per se including the Indian Defence procurement process. Besides, it also includes the bureaucratic structure, their financial powers and adminstrative powers including their contact details. Similarly details of the other major stake holders i.e., the trade have also been compiled to the extent possible and placed appropriately in the book. Hopefully this book will provide both the buyers as well as the sellers, including their Indian partners a one stop guide answering all that they wish to know.

Gp Capt Sanjiv Aggarwal

Chapter – I

DEFENCE PROCUREMENT PROCEDURE

Introduction

India's Defence Budget has increased substantially over the years, from Rs. 157.50 billion in 1990-91 to Rs 1473.44 billion in 2010-11. The latest defence budget accounts for nearly 13% of total Central Government expenditure, and around 2.1% of GDP. In order to ensure better management of public money and procure defence equipments in shortest possible time, the Ministry of Defence (MoD) has evolved, over the years, a 'fast and transparent' defence procurement policy, which is articulated in a document known as Defence Procurement Procedure (DPP). The document is revised periodically (now in every year) so as to meet the legimitate requirements of various stakeholders and facilitate expeditious acquisition, based on the feedback that the MoD receives from various concerned agencies.

Evolution of Defence Procurement Procedure — A Brief History

Defence equipment is generally very expensive and requires huge investments. It was, therefore, felt by the Government of India that proper procedures be laid down which should be strictly adhered to for all procurements so as to derive best value of money. Well formulated procedures not only help in ensuring expeditious procurement of the approved equipment in terms of capabilities but also ensure its procurement within time-frame prescribed by optimally utilizing the allocated budgetary resources.

Emphasizing the need for well formulated procedure for defence procurement, the Public Accounts Committee (PAC), Lok Sabha (The lower house of Indian Parliament), in their 187th Report (1989) recommended that Government should draw up comprehensive guidelines with regard to negotiations and implementation of defence contracts.

Defence Procurement Procedure 1992 (DPP-1992)

Based on the above recommendation of PAC, the MoD issued guidelines for all procurement cases involving an outlay of Rs 0.10 billion or more in February 1992. It is commonly referred to as Defence Procurement Procedure 1992 (DPP-1992). Modifications were incorporated in it from time to time. DPP-1992 laid down the steps to be followed for the complete gamut of procurement process. Though DPP-1992 was a creditable effort as it covered all the activities pertaining to procurement, it suffered from several inadequacies which became apparent in its implementation over the years. Some of the deficiencies in DPP-1992 were:

- It did not cater to emergent requirements.
- A major grey area pertained to Transfer of Technology under 'Buy and Make' category.
- Single-stage two bid system was not adequately stressed upon. Therefore, in a number of cases commercial quotes were sought from a single vendor after successful completion of trials.
- It did not provide for an in-built review mechanism.
- A large number of agencies were involved in the process, yet there was no single monitoring agency.
- After the finalization of Services Qualitative Requirements, Defence Research and Development Organisation (DRDO) was generally given the first option to develop the equipment. Vetting by DRDO entailed additional time.

- The procedure did not cater for long-duration projects.
- There was no dedicated organization meant exclusively for procurement purposes. Most of the officers held multiple charges thus dividing their attention and efforts.

The shortcomings became more apparent during the Kargil conflict in 1999 when emergent procurements were required to be made. After the Kargil conflict, the Government of India constituted a Group of Ministers (GOM) to go into the entire gamut of national security. The GOM Report, which was submitted in February, 2001, noted *inter alia* that the existing structure for procurement had led to sub-optimal utilization of funds, long delays in acquisition and had not been conducive to the modernization of the Services. They suggested for creation of a separate and dedicated institutional structure and establishment of Defence Procurement Organisation (DPO). Consequent to the GOM recommendations, the MoD established a new Defence Procurement Organization in October 2001. The GOM report also led to broad guidelines for the new defence procurement procedure which was promulgated in 2002.

Defence Procurement Procedure 2002

Defence Procurement Procedure 2002, which was promulgated in December 2002 was applicable for procurements flowing out of 'Buy' decision of Defence Acquisition Council (DAC), the highest decision making body in the MoD. This procedure was subsequently amended in June 2003 to include procurement on 'Buy and Make' through Imported Transfer of Technology (TOT) and termed as DPP-2002 (Version June 2003). The June 2003 Version laid the acquisition procedure in eleven standard processes such as:

1. Services Qualitative Requirements (SQRs)
2. Acceptance of Necessity,
3. Solicitation of Offers,
4. Evaluation of Technical offers by Technical Evaluation Committee (TEC),

5. Field Evaluation,
6. Staff Evaluation,
7. Oversight by Technical Oversight Committee (TOC),
8. Commercial Negotiations by Contract Negotiation Committee (CNC),
9. Oversight by Eminent Persons Group,
10. Award of Contract/Supply Order (SO),
11. Contract Administration and post-contract management.

The standard procedures and requirements for each of these stages are discussed and enumerated in Chapter III covering the complete acquisition procedure in the Armed Forces of India.

The DPP 2003 (version June 03) was an improvement over the DPP-1992 and DPP-2002 in many ways. However, with the passage of time, few shortcomings became apparent, having bearing on time and cost of procured items. The procedures did not provide *inter alia* any timeframe for each stage of acquisition, resulting in undue delay in procurement. The tendering of defence items, including even many non-sensitive items, was conducted in secrecy, leading to single vendor situations in most cases. It also did not provide any provision for detailed objective financial assessment with respect to exchange rate variation and 'Discounted Cash Flow'. The procedure also did not address the need for formulation of joint QRs for items common to three Services.

Defence Procurement Procedure 2005 (DPP-2005)

To further streamline the acquisition procedure and to incorporate the suggestions received from the Central Vigilance Commission and Comptroller and Auditor General, the MoD came out with a new procurement procedure in 2005. The new defence procurement procedure sought to broad base QRs to generate maximum vendor response; introduced open tendering for commercially off-the-shelf (COTS) items. It also introduced for the first time; Integrity

Pact and Offsets provisions for items worth over Rs. 3.00 billion. Provision was made for the preparation of Joint Services Qualitative Requirements for common items of the three Services. Objective financial evaluation was made part of the procedure. Broad timeframe for each of the activities was prescribed for the time bound completion of acquisition process (see **Annexure-I**).

Defence Procurement Procedure 2006 (DPP-2006)

To further improve the procurement procedure, the MoD announced DPP-2006 in August 2006. The DPP-2006, which became operational since September 2006, made a number of new initiatives like collegiate decision making by the DAC, procedure for Integrity Pact and Defence Offsets was put in place. Level playing field was created for domestic private players; clear timeframe for each acquisition process was spelt out. The new procedure, for the first time, issued detailed guidelines for 'Make' category aimed at promoting 'indigenous research, design, development and production' of defence systems. To step up transparency and competition, vendors are allowed to register themselves through internet. The procedure for trial and evaluation has further been streamlined for increased transparency.

Defence Procurement Procedure 2008 (DPP-2008)

Based on the feedback during the time DPP-2006's was in vogue, the MoD announced DPP-2008 in August 2008. The new version, which came into operation since September 2008, brought about a number of improvements over the DPP-2006. These improvements include: broad details of the trial methodology to form part of the RFP so that vendors are, at the outset aware of the modalities by which their product will be evaluated. Directions to vendors during the course of trials and the results of the evaluations along with the reasons for disqualifications, if any, will be communicated in writing and placed on record. On the offset policy, the

DPP-2008 included a provision for offset credit banking with the hope that the said provision will enable foreign participants to create offset programmes, in anticipation, of future obligations. The earlier mandatory requirement of an industrial license for a domestic firm to participate in such offset was relaxed so that all that they now need to do is to meet the relevant guidelines specified by the Ministry of Commerce and Industry.

Amendments to DPP-2008

In July 2009, the Defence Minister informed the Parliament that DPP would be revised on an annual basis, instead of every two years, which was the practice earlier. In keeping with the above promise, the MoD brought certain amendments to the DPP-2008. The Amendments, brought into force since November 01, 2009, introduced the following provisions:

1. Introduction of new category for acquisition 'Buy & Make (Indian)'
2. Sharing of information with Indian Industry.
3. Enhancing role of Independent Monitors.
4. Removal of ambiguity regarding Earnest Money Deposit (EMD) in signing the Integrity Pact.
5. Formulation of SQRs including issue of Request for Information (RFI).
6. Offsets requirement in 'Option Clause' cases and change of offset partner in exceptional cases.

Defence Procurements Procedure 2011 (DPP-2011)

In early January 2011, the MoD issued the revised DPP. The DPP-2011, which supersedes DPP-2008 and its 2009 Amendments, has come into effect from January 01, 2011. The new document brought about the following changes:

1. In an effort to ensure that Indian private sector is placed at par with the Defence Public Sector Undertakings (DPSUS), the Exchange Rate Variation clause has now been made applicable to all Indian vendors when they compete with their foreign counterparts under the "Buy Global" category.
2. Bank Guarantees under the Integrity Pact have now been linked to the validity of the Commercial Offer submitted by vendors and are, therefore, no longer open ended, as the case earlier.
3. The requirement of furnishing two separate financial bonds for performance of contract and warranty of equipment has now been amalgamated into a single Performance-cum-Warranty Bond. This is a step towards easing the administrative and financial burden on Indian defence manufacturers.
4. The stringent clause for blacklisting vendors for delay in delivery of equipment, in fast track procurement cases has been removed. However, the liquidated damages have been marginally enhanced to ensure greater accountability by vendors.

In addition to above, the DPP also made certain changes in its shipbuilding procedure and expanded the scope of defence products for purpose of discharge of offset obligations. As regards shipbuilding, the Chapter-III of DPP-2011 is divided into two sections of guidelines, in comparison to the one set of guidelines in DPP-2008. Section A of Chapter-III of DPP-2011 incorporates the provisions which would be applicable exclusively for the government-owned shipyards on nomination basis, while the provisions in Section B are meant more or less for private shipyards—although they equally apply to state-owned shipyards—on competitive basis. The Defence Ministry hopes that the Section B would "encourage participation of the private shipyards and promote indigenisation and self-reliance in warship construction."

The refinement to the offset provision is in terms of expansion of the list of products which could be resorted to by the foreign companies for discharging their offset obligations. The earlier" List of Defence Products" has been expanded under the new name "List of Products Eligible for Discharge of Offset Obligations" to include products of two more categories: "Products for Internal Security" and "Civil Aerospace Product". In all, the DPP-2011 has 27 categories of products (in comparison to 13 categories in DPP-2008), which could be used for offsets purpose.

It is noteworthy that the revised product list in DPP-2011 is exclusive of certain service which could also be resorted to by the foreign companies to discharge their mandatory offset obligations. As per the revised guidelines, "for the purpose of discharge of offsets, 'services' will mean maintenance, overhaul, upgradation, life extension, engineering, design, testing of eligible products as indicated in [the expanded eligible product list] and training. Training may include training services and training equipment (e.g. simulators) but exclude civil infrastructure. "The MoD is optimistic that the expanded product list and inclusion of services and training in the offset ambit "will provide a wider range of offset opportunities to vendors participating in defence procurements and encourage building up of indigenous manufacturing in crucial areas."

The recent changes with respect to DPP-2008 are sumrised in a tabular form below to enable everybody to understand the implications of these changes.

DPP-2008	Changes in DPP-2011	Remarks
Para 20 of Chapter I: Acceptance of Necessity (AON) would lapse where the RFP for approved quantity is not normal within two years from accord of AON	*Para 20 of Chapter I:* For cases where the original RFP has been issued within two years from accord of AON and later retracted for any reason, the AON would continue to remain valid, as long as the original decision and categorisation remain unchanged, provided the subsequent RFP is issued within one year from the date of retraction of original RFP	The extension of validity would save processing time, which is quite significant given the file movements across cross sections of decision/approval points within the Armed Forces and MoD.

DPP-2008	Changes in DPP-2011	Remarks
Para 28 of Chapter I: For transfer of technology (ToT) from foreign companies to Indian companies for maintenance infrastructure, the Indian firms would be DPSUs/OFB/Raksha Udyog Ratnas (RUR) or any other firms as selected by the Department of Defence Production.	*Para 28 of Chapter I:* The Indian entity could be a company incorporated under The Companies Act 1956, including DPSUs or entities like CFB/Army Base Workshops/ Naval Dockyards/Base Repair Depots of Air Force.	For the private sector, the deletion of RURs in the revised para leaves the chance of getting in to maintenance business to those companies who are registered under the Companies Act. The nomination approach could be a hindrance in the getting.
Para 41 of Chapter I: Any vendor failing to produce equipment for trials by due date would normally be given a grace period of 15 days to produce the equipment for trials. However, if the equipment is not evaluated in the initial trials then the vendor/ equipment would not be considered at a later point of time.	*Para 41 of Chapter I:* Any vendor failing to produce equipment for trials by due date would normally be given a grace period of 15 days to produce the equipment for trials. An additional grace period of up to 30 days may be obtained by Service Headquarters from their respective Vice Chief keeping in view the practical time period necessary for trials.	The extension of grace period may retain participation of some companies who have genuine difficultly in fielding their equipments in the originally stipulated time period.
Para 46 of Chapter –I: The Technical Oversight Committee (TOC) will comprise of 3 members, one Service Officer, one DRDO scientist and one representative of DPSU not involved with that acquisition	*Para 46 of Chapter I:* A TOC will comprise three members- one Service Officer, one DRDO scientist and one representative of DPSU. Members nominated should have adequate seniority and experience and should not be involved with that acquisition case.	Senior and experienced members in TOC would provide better oversight.
Annexure III to Appendix F (Guidelines of protection of Exchange Rate Variation (ERV) in Contracts with Defence PSUs): Defence PSUs are allowed to insert ERV clause in both 'Buy (Global)' and 'Buy (Indian)' contracts	*Annexure III to Appendix F (Guidelines of Protection of Exchange Rate Variation in Contracts):* Indian vendors are allowed to insert ERV clause in 'Buy (Global)' cases. They are not allowed to insert the clause in 'Buy (Indian)' contracts, unless the supplier	The new ERV guidelines are a step towards creating level playing field between Indian private and public sector companies.

DPP-2008	Changes in DPP-2011	Remarks
	is a defence PSU in ab-initio single vendor cases or when nominated as production agency	
Paras 7 and 8 of Appendix F to Schedule I (Payment Terms): Separate Performance and Warranty Bonds, each amounting to five per cent of value of the contract to be submitted by the seller	*Para 7 of Appendix F to Schedule I (Payment Terms):* The seller is required to give only one Performance cum Warranty Bond of five per cent of the value of the contract.	This would halve the financial burden on the seller, which may be reflected in its commercial quote
	Para 3 (p) Timeline for Procurement (Security Classification): In case of deviations to the timelines gives at Appendix C to Chapter 1 of DPP, such deviations and week-wise targets to be proposed by SHQ with justification in a new format.	The insertion of new para will bring higher accountability among acquisition functionaries
Appendix C (Refers to Para 74 (a) of Chapter I): Month-wise broad timeframe for completion difference procurement activities.	*Appendix C (Refers to Para 74 (a) of Chapter I):* Week-wise broad timeframe for completion difference procurement activities.	The week-wise timeframe provides a better picture of time taken by various procurement agencies. It would also help bring more accountability.
Para 27 of Chapter IV (Liquidated Damages – Fast Track Procedure): In case of delay of supplies, the vendor will run the risk of imposition of LD (Liquidated Damages) @ 1% per week subject to maximum of 10% of value of delayed store apart from the getting black listed and debarred from future dealing with Government of India.	*Para 27 of Chapter IV (Liquidated Damages):* In case of delay of supplies, the vendor will run the risk of imposition of LD @ 1.5% per week subject to maximum of 15% of value of delayed store.	The omission of reference to blacklisting could be a tacit understanding of MoD that such option does not bring higher accountability on the part of vendors. The increase of value of LD as an alternative to blacklisting is more pragmatic.

Defence Production Policy

Beginning this year i.e. January 2011, the Government of India has for the first time articulated its defence production policy. The primary objective of this policy is to achieve self-reliance in the development and production of weapon systems and platforms. This policy in the long run will have its effect on the procurement decisions as well as on the kind of offsets that is desirable to meet this broad objective. The policy document in full is given at end of the book in Annexure 9.

Categories of Defence Capital Acquisitions

As per DPP, defence capital acquisition is divided into the following four broad categories:

- **'Buy':** This means an outright purchase of equipment. Based on the source of procurement, the category is classified as 'Buy (Indian)' and 'Buy (Global)'. 'Indian' means Indian vendors only and 'Global' means foreign as well as Indian vendors. 'Buy Indian' must have minimum 30% indigenous content if the systems are being integrated by an Indian vendor.
- **'Buy & Make':** Acquisitions covered under the 'Buy & Make' decision would mean purchase from a foreign vendor followed by licensed production/indigenous manufacture in the country.
- **'Make':** Acquisitions covered under the 'Make' decision would include high technology complex systems to be designed, developed and produced indigenously.
- **'Buy & Make (Indian)':** Acquisitions covered under the 'Buy & Make (Indian)' decision would mean purchase from an Indian vendor including an Indian company forming joint venture/establishing production arrangement with OEM followed by licensed production/indigenous manufacture in the country. 'Buy & Make (Indian)' must have minimum 50% indigenous content on cost basis.

Acquisition Process for 'Buy' and 'Buy & Make'

The acquisition process for schemes categorised as 'Buy' and 'Buy & Make' with ToT is done in eleven different stages as enumerated in page number 17 already. The detailed process at each of these stages has been amplified in Chapter III.

Organisational Structure for Defence Capital Acquisition

Following the recommendation of GOM Report, the MoD has set up a Defence Procurement Organisation (DPO). The constituents of this are depicted as below:

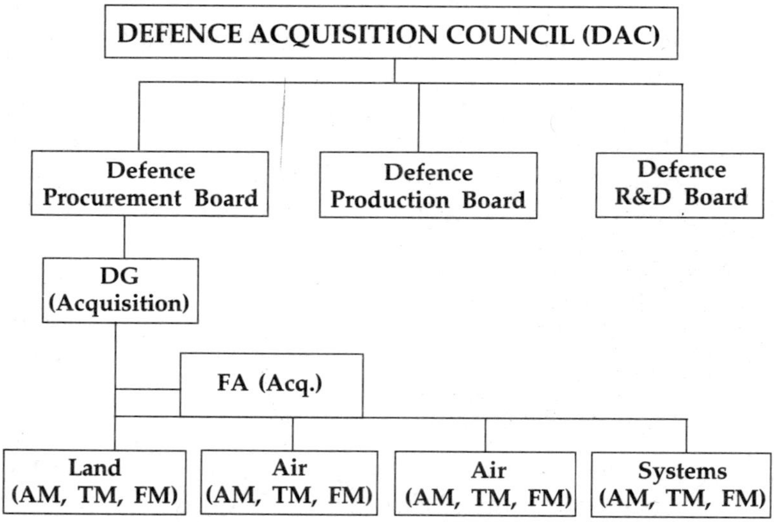

Defence Acquisition Council (DAC)

It is an overarching structure under the Union Defence Minister. It consists of Minister of Defence for State, Chief of Army Staff (COAS), Chief of Naval Staff (CNS), Chief of Air Staff (CAS), Defence Secretary, Secretary, Defence Production (DP), Secretary Research & Development (R&D), Secretary (Defence Finance), Chief of Integrated Defence

Staff (CIDS) and Special Secretary (Acquisition). DAC has been asked to give in principle approval to capital acquisitions in the Long Term Perspective Plan (LTPP) covering a 15 year time span at the beginning of a Five year Plan period. It also approved all capital acquisition projects, identifying them as 'Buy', 'Buy&Make', 'Make', 'Buy & Make (India)' cases. Monitoring the progress of major projects is also its responsibility. The decisions of Defence Minister based on DAC deliberations flows down for implementation to Defence Procurement Board, Defence Production Board and Defence R&D Board.

Defence Procurement Board (DPB)

It functions under the Defence Secretary and has Secretary (Defence Production), Secretary (Defence Research & Development), Secretary (Defence Finance), Vice Chiefs of the three Services and Special Secretary (Acquisition) as members. It oversees all activities related to 'Buy' and 'Buy and Make' decisions of DAC. It is responsible for the coordination, supervision and monitoring of the acquisition process. It has also been tasked to examine proposals from the Acquisition Wing regarding procurement procedures and make necessary changes in the procurement process after obtaining the approval of Raksha Mantri.

Defence Production Board

It functions under Secretary (DP) and oversees all activities related to the indigenous manufacture under the Department of Defence Production flowing from the 'Buy and Make' and 'Make' decisions of the DAC.

Defence R&D Board

It is chaired by Secretary (Def. R&D) and is responsible to progress, monitor and report on all indigenous proposals flowing out of the 'Buy and Make' and 'Make' decisions of the DAC.

Acquisition Wing

The Defence Procurement Board is assisted in its functioning by an Acquisition Wing in the Department of Defence. All matters concerning acquisition of capital nature are dealt with by it. It is an integrated set up with officers from the Department of Defence, Finance Division and Service Headquarters (SHQs). It is headed by Additional/ Special Secretary (Acquisition) and is assisted by Financial Adviser (Acquisition) who also functions as the Integrated Financial Adviser and heads the Finance Branch in the Acquisition Wing. The Wing consists of four Divisions – Land, Maritime, Air Force and Systems. Each Division has a Joint Secretary (JS) designated as Acquisition Manager, an Addl. Financial Adviser designated as Finance Manager and a Service Officer of two-star rank designated as Technical Manager.

"Our objective is to focus on the centrality of national interests in the conduct of our external relations and the pursuit of our economic interests. We have taken important initiatives, keeping in mind the imperatives of retaining our freedom of options, remaining alive to our concerns"

Dr. Manmohan Singh
Prime Minister of India
in Parliament

Chapter – 2

Defence Procurement Process in India

Lieutenant General Henry T Glisson, US Army, has said that as the modern warfare increases technical sophistication speed and complexity, there will be dramatic changes to the way we fight. These changes in 'how we fight' will require a change in the way we provide support. Acquisition Organisations and systems must change accordingly to keep with this pace. These changes are slowly getting evolved in the current Defence Procurement Policy of India. Indian bureaucracy is a minefield of regulations, regulators and legislations. The Indian Defence Forces on the other hand are complex in nature with nearly 2.8 million combatants and civilians. It is therefore necessary for the prospective organizations venturing to enter this complex Indian market to have an in depth knowledge of the Government Procurement Process and procedures and as to how the capital budget is actually spent in India.

Perspective Planning Process

Like in any other Defence Forces, all across the world, planning in India is also based on long, medium and short term perspective. Accordingly, the acquisition plans are made from long term (15 years), medium term (5 years) and short term (annual/two years roll on) perspectives. The long term plans are made by HQ Integrated Defence Staff and Service HQ together from which the medium and annual plans are drawn.

The complete planning process is undertaken under the guidance of Defence Acquisition Council and is approved by the Minister of Defence. The implementation of these plans is overseen by Defence Procurement Board (DPB). Whereas the Long Term Integrated Procurement Plans (LTIPP) and Services Capability Plans (SCAP) are approved by the Defence Acquisition Council (DAC), the Annual Acquisition Plan (AAP) which is a subset of SCAP is approved by the DPB. The organizational structure of the DAC is already given in Chapter 1. The planning process flow chart is given below for easy comprehension.

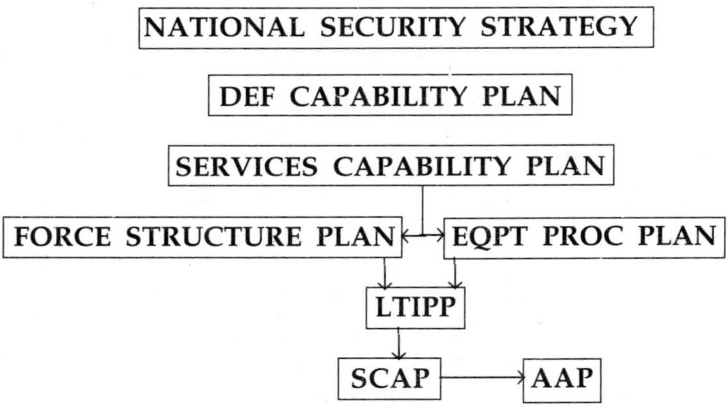

Once the respective plans are approved, the process of actual acquisition commences. It follows different stages. The flow and process during these stages has been amplified in succeeding paragraphs. The time taken for each activity is also set down in terms of weeks. Same is given in Annexure I.

Stage 1 – Drawing of Service Qualitative Requirements (SQRs)

- These lay down users requirements in a comprehensive and structured manner. These are broad based and realistic.
- These express the user's requirements in terms of functional characteristics and are drafted by the user directorate at Service HQs.

- Prior to their approval, Staff Equipment Policy Group (SEPC) assess whether it will result in multi-vendor situation. In case, a single vendor situation is likely, then the reasons for formulation of such SQRs are recorded or are changed to broader characteristics to ensure larger participation.
- Approved SQRs are required to be of a contemporary technology widely available in the world/indigenous market and its performance parameters should be verifiable and classified as 'essential parameters'.
- There are no 'desirable parameters' in the SQRs.
- Waiver of SQR parameters can only be accorded by the Service HQ concerned before issue of RFP. Thereafter, no waivers of parameters are granted.

Stage 2 – Acceptance of Necessity

- Service HQ put up Statement of Cases as per the format given in DPP and submit it to DDP, DRDO, MoD (Fin) and Administrative branch of MoD.
- It includes total quantities required, the break up based on five years plan and the quantity that is required to be procured in the next two years.
- Quantity vetting is recommended by the administrative branch in consultation with MoD (Fin) and thereafter the case is sent back to Service HQ for further processing.
- The SOC is then placed before categorization committee for the recommended quantities to be acquired, categorization and for acceptance of necessity for final approval of DAC/DPP.
- For cases where the original RFP has been issued within two years from accord of AON and later retracted for any reason, the AON would continue to remain valid, as long as the original decision and categorisation

remain unchanged, provided the subsequent RFP is issued within one year from the date of retraction of original RFP.

Stage 3 – Solicitation of Offers

- Shortlisting of prospective manufacturers/suppliers is done by Service HQ.
- Primarily all the OEMs/authorized vendors/ Government sponsored export agencies are included.
- Technical managers in acquisition wing are required to maintain a databank.
- Appropriate publicity can be given to the proposed procurement with a view to generate maximum competition through Internet, MoD website, Newspapers etc.
- Offers are generally called in single stage two bid system.
- RFP is issued soliciting the technical and commercial offers together but in two separate sealed envelopes.

Stage 4 – Technical Evaluation Committee (TEC)

- It is constituted by respective Service HQs for evaluation of the technical bids with respect to SQRs as given in the RFPs.
- It has representatives of user service, maintenance agencies, QA, DRDO, etc.
- It examines extent of variation in technical characteristics of the equipment offered by the suppliers and prepares a 'compliance statement' short listing the equipment for trials/induction.
- It may invite vendors for technical presentations, if needed.

- A technical offer, once submitted, cannot be materially changed subsequently.

Stage 5 – Field Evaluation Trials

- These are carried out by user service on the basis of standard operating procedures.
- Manufacturers of short listed equipment are asked to send desired number of equipment/weapon systems to India.
- Service HQ formulates trial directive and constitute a trial team.
- SQRs are part of trial directive.
- Parameters not mentioned in RFP are not considered.
- Validation of Support system and maintainability trials are done simultaneously and after each stage of trials, a debriefing of all the vendors is done.
- Field evaluation is conducted by users in all conditions where the equipment is likely to be deployed.
- Vendors failing to produce equipment for trials by due date can be given a grace time up to 15 days. An additional grace period of up to 30 days may be obtained by Service Headquarters from their respective Vice Chief keeping in view the practical time period necessary for trials
- Field evaluation report is drawn up and sent to Service HQ for preparation of Staff evaluation.
- Generally following types of trials are carried out. The trials are generally carried on NCNC basis
  - (a) Technical trials by DRDO or DGQA to assess technical suitability.
  - (b) User trials carried out on prototypes under simulated operational conditions to confirm a suitability for introduction into service.

(c) Troop trials to assess combat effectiveness of critical equipment required in large numbers.

(d) Combined user-cum-technical trials are done as an exception when trial stores are not available in requisite numbers or the equipment is required urgently.

(e) Maintainability evaluation trials are carried out for all maintainability aspects.

(f) Accelerated user-cum-reliability trials are undertaken for data collection on reliability, preventive maintenance, equipment life, engineering support plan and maintenance scales.

Stage 6 – Staff Evaluation

- Based on the field evaluation trials and the report, Service HQ carry out a staff evaluation.
- It compares compliance of demonstrated performance of equipment vis-à-vis SQRs.
- They analyse field evaluation results and shortlist equipment recommended. The evaluation report is approved by Service HQ and is forwarded to Acquisition Wing for acceptance.
- If no vendor meets SQRs in field evaluation, then the case is foreclosed and a fresh RFP issued after reformulating the SQRs.
- Waivers/amendments to SQRs can be sought only for 'Make' projects of DRDO/OFB/DPSUs/Private Industry.

Stage 7 – Technical oversight Committee (ToC)

- It provides expert oversight over technical evaluation.
- It generally comprises of 3 members– 1 Service officer, 1 DRDO scientist and 1 rep of public sector undertaking not involved with the acquisition.

- Members nominated should have adequate seniority and experience and should not be involved with that acquisition case.
- It is tasked to see whether trials, trial evaluations, compliance to QRs and selection of vendors was done according to prescribed procedures.
- The ruling is based on a majority decision to be submitted within 30 days.
- Absence of a response within this period is deemed to be acceptance.

Stage 8 – Commercial Negotiations by Contract Negotiating Committee (CNC)

- Commercial negotiations commence after Staff evaluation report is accepted by DG Acquisition and ToC report accepted by Defence Secretary.
- CNC carry out all process right from opening of commercial bids till conclusion of contract.
- Sealed commercial offers of only technically accepted vendors are opened by CNC at a predetermined date and time under intimation to all concerned vendors.
- Comparative statement of tenders is drawn to determine L1 vendor and once L1 vendor is identified, the contract is concluded with him. There would be no need for further price negotiations unless there are exceptional circumstances and where valid logical reasons exist. Such negotiations are held only with L1 vendor.
- The standard composition of CNC is as follows:

  Acquisition Manager, Chairman.

  Technical Manager.

  Finance Manager.

  Advisor Cost.

DGQA representative.

Procurement agency representative.

User representative.

Representation of Contract Management branch at SHQ.

Representation from repair agency.

Under Secretary concerned.

Member Secretary to be nominated by the Chairman.

If TOT, then Representation of DRDO/production agency.

If offsets is part of the contract, then rep of DOFA is included.

Stage 9 – Approval of CFA

- All CNC documents leading to selection of vendor with a formal written recommendation report is forwarded to the competent financial authority based on the cost of acquisition.
- The method of evaluation and rationale for the final selection made is explained elaborately.
- CNC report is processed by Acquisition Manager for obtaining expenditure clearance and CFA approval.

Stage 10 – Award of Contract/Supply order

- Once the approval of CFA is given, the supply order is given to the successful vendor.

Stage 11 – Post Contract Monitoring

- Responsibility for Contract administration and management rests with respective Service HQ.
- Post Contract Monitoring is the responsibility of respective Acquisition Wings.

- Phased reviews are carried out on the progress of the Contract by a steering committee generally headed by DG Acquisition or by a PSO at Service HQ.

Classification of Types of Procurements in India

It is necessary to understand that how different types of procurement is classified in India so as to get clarity as to how money gets actually consumed under different heads of accounts. Procurement is classified in six different ways as per the following terminology:

(a) **Capital Procurement:** Expenditure under this head shall be with the object of acquiring tangible assets of a permanent nature or for enhancing the utility of the existing assets.

(b) **Revenue Procurement:** Expenditure under this head implies procurement of items and equipment including replacement equipment to maintain and operate already sanctioned assets in the service.

(c) **Indigenous Procurement:** All procurement from indigenous sources are classified as indigenous procurement.

(d) **Foreign Procurement:** Procurement against such Defence equipment and assets which are of foreign origin including items required to maintain and operate which may also be required to be procured from suppliers abroad.

(e) **Central Procurement:** Procurement taken against indents resulting from land provisioning process.

(f) **Local Procurement:** To meet the short term, adhoc or urgent requirements when supplies are not available through the Central provisioning agency or are not within the purview of central purchase organization.

Out of the six categories explained above, what matters in our context is capital procurement and foreign procurement for which guidelines have been given in relevant portions of the DPP and other financial rules and regulations.

Financial Powers

Like in any organization, financial powers have been delegated at various levels. Service HQ have been given the power of procurement upto Rs. 50 crores under the Capital head. Beyond that the delegation is as follows:

Service HQ	-	50 crores
Defence Secretary	-	0–75 crores
DPB	-	Upto 100 crores
Raksha Mantri	-	Upto 200 crores
Raksha Mantri & Finance Minister	-	Upto 500 crores
CCS	-	Above 500 crores

This chapter has been deliberately included in the book, despite the fact that in the context of offsets, it has limited use. This is done to ensure that the stakeholders understand and assimilate the total procurement process in India; offsets of which is but a subset. This will give them a complete overview of the Indian political as well as Administrative setup and will hopefully prepare them better in unravelling and countering different situations which are part and parcel of doing business in this side of the world.

Chapter – 3

DEFENCE OFFSETS

Definition

As per the definition of Bureau of Industry and Security (of US Department of Commerce), offsets are defined as "Compensation practices required as a condition of purchase in either government-to-government or commercial sales of 'defence articles' and/or 'defence services'. Defence offsets are further divided into two categories: Direct Offsets and Indirect Offsets. Direct offsets are the contractual arrangements that involve defence articles and services referenced in the sales agreement for military exports. These transactions are directly related to the defence items or services exported by the defence firm and are usually in the form of co-production, subcontracting, technology transfer, training, production, licensed production, or financing activities.

On the other hand, indirect offsets are the contractual arrangements that involve defence goods and services unrelated to the defence items or services export referenced in the sales agreement. The kinds of offsets that are considered "indirect" include purchases, investment, training, financing activities, marketing/exporting assistance, and technology transfer.

Forms of Offsets

Co-production

When the offsets take the form of co-production, it involves the buyer's right to produce all or a part of the procured item.

Licensed Production

In this case the buyer obtains technical information from the supplier to license produce the intended product.

Technology Transfer

It involves an agreement which leads to transfer of know-how and know-why to a foreign country.

Sub-contracts

It involves overseas production of a part or component of a defence article.

Purchases

Procurement of off-the-shelf items from the offset recipient.

Some Concepts in Defence Offsets

Multiplier

A factor applied to the actual value of certain offsets transactions to calculate the credit value earned. Foreign governments use multipliers to provide firms with incentives to offer offsets in targeted areas of economic growth. When a multiplier is applied to the off-the-shelf price of a more desirable service or product offered as an offset, the defence firm receives a higher credit value toward fulfilling an offset obligation.

Example: A foreign government interested in a specific technology may offer a multiplier of "six" for offset transactions providing access to that technology. A UK defence company with a 120 per cent offset obligation from a $1 million sale of defence systems ordinarily would be required to provide technology transfer through an offset equalling $1.2 million. With a multiplier of six, however, the UK company could offer only $200,000 (actual value) in technology transfer and earn $1.2 million in credit value, fulfilling its entire offset obligation under the agreement.

Why Multiplier

Countries often provide multipliers towards the fulfilment of offset obligation by the foreign companies. Foreign companies see multipliers as inducements as it raises the credit value of offsets, and thus reduces the "dollar value" of their obligations. The buyer countries, on the other hand, use this as a tool to engage companies in certain type of activities that they view important for their industrial or overall economic development. For instance, Denmark offers multiplier of maximum of 10 but restricts it to few cases such as R&D, Technology transfer, among others. Globally the range of multipliers vary from as low as zero (as in the case of Australia, Canada, etc) to as high as 30 as is case with the Netherlands. However, according to the BIS database, over the years the percentage use of multipliers applied in offset transaction are on a continuous declining trend, coming down from 16.6 per cent in 1993 to 4.3 per cent in 2006. The reason behind this decline though is not clear, yet it suggests, inter alia, countries decreasing preference for multiplier as a useful tool. Nonetheless, higher multipliers are desired in training, overseas investment, technology transfer and licensed production.

Offset Credit Banking

The provision of offset credit banking in the procurement policy allows foreign participants to accumulate offset credits from previous investments for discharging future obligations. The foreign supplier while view it useful as it reduces their obligation for a particular contract by taking the advantage of the earlier investments, the stringent provisions within the policy gives little freedom in making full use of such parked credits. The recent modified Danish offset policy related to banking of offset credit restricts the foreign suppliers to the "new or continued cooperation" with the host companies. The Danish policy requires the foreign vendors to get approval from the government for parking credits from the ongoing contracts that could be valid for use for the next five years. In addition, it makes it mandatory that "banked credits" cannot be used to fulfil the minimum required 30 per cent offset and multipliers could not be used for such credit banking agreement. However, for a specific contract for which bidder prepares for winning, multipliers, up to 10, and banked credits can be utilised. The aim of the Danish offset policy is to "engage foreign suppliers in a new or continuous cooperation" with the domestic companies.

Defence Offsets: Global Trend & Strategies

On theoretical and empirical grounds there is so far little evidence to advocate for offsets in defence trade. In practice, however, offset is an integral part of international defence trade and, over 70 countries use it as discriminating factor in their arms contracts. To some, offset is 'a positive development tool' and the "companies that plan for this are successful and able to investigate the potential for strategic partnerships." The volume of offset and its greater percentage applicability in arms contracts speaks for itself. Though the exact value of global defence offsets is not readily available, some idea can be formed from the data provided by the US Department of Commerce's Bureau of Industry and Statistics (BIS) which tracks the offset obligations of the US defence contractors. As per the latest BIS Report, during the 14-year period from 1993 to 2006, the US entered into offset agreements with 42 countries; with total value (of all offset agreements) amounting more than $60 billion, or over 71 per cent of agreed export value. In 2006 alone, it signed 44 offset agreements worth nearly $3.5 billion with 12 companies from 20 countries.

With time, the percentage demand for offsets – though it still varies from region to region and country to country – has increased significantly. It is because countries that did not "require offset during pre-1990s now require them as routine policy" and, some countries have increased their demands over a period of time. In the above mentioned 14-year period, the US, has witnessed the offset percentage of its defence trade increasing, on an average, from 34.3 per cent in 1993 to nearly 125 per cent in 2003, before decreasing to some 71per cent in 2006. Region-wise, European countries with an average offset demand of 98.4 per cent during the above period are ahead of North and South America (97%), Middle East and Africa (44%), and Asia Pacific (39.1%). A 3-year moving average of offsets demanded (in percentage terms) from the US defence contractors is shown in the Figure-1 below.

Figure-1

Offset Percentage in US's Defence Trade, 1993-2006

(3-Year Moving Average)

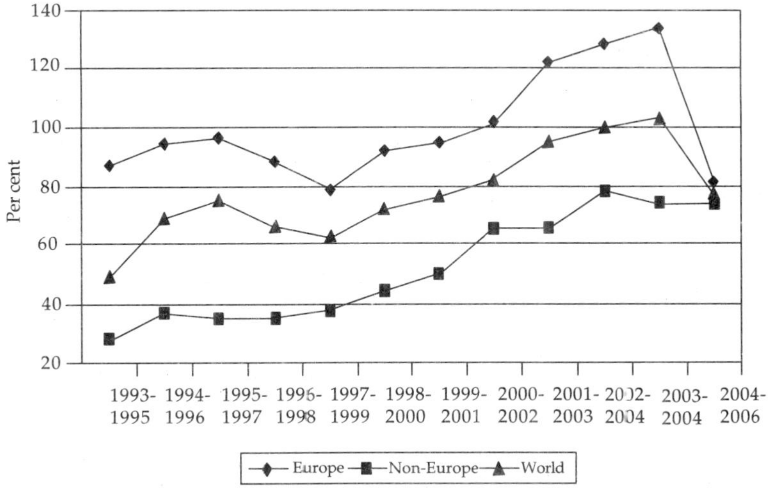

Note: Extrapolated from Table 4-2: Offset Agreement: Europe Compared to the Rest of World 1993-2006

Source: BIS Offsets database, as cited in the US Department of Commerce, Bureau of Industry and Security, *Offsets in Defence Trade: Twelfth Report to Congress*, December 2007, p. 4-7.

While the inter-regional difference in the offset requirements can largely be ascribed to the varying level of industrial development in these regions, it is the same difference that could be the factor behind the progressive increase in demands by the Non-European countries. For instance, among the non-European countries, South Korea and Taiwan have increased their average offset demands from the US companies, from 36.6 per cent and 18.4 per cent during 1993-1999 to 63.7 per cent and 48.7 per cent, respectively during 2000-2006. Moreover, these two countries offsets are confined to the defence sector unlike most of their European countries who prefer both defence and civil-specific offsets. The growing aspiration among the countries, reflected in the increasing offset requirements, can be seen in the context of their desire in "obtaining valuable technology, and manufacturing know-how, supporting domestic employment, creating or expanding their defence industries, and making the use of their national funds ... more politically palatable.

Though countries have yet to prove the efficacy of offsets in its totality, nonetheless, there are few instances where countries using offsets have become competent enough to compete against their offset providers. The above success may be limited to few select companies or countries, yet as the 14-year trend suggests, countries would continue to look for more opportunities in various forms of assistance, from the external sources.

In addition to the above, countries use mixed strategies within the policy to achieve their desired objectives. A selected list of strategies of offset policy of 10 countries is at the end of this chapter. As the offset policies of 10 countries reveal that the minimum threshold of offset value of defence contract is as low as $ 0.5 million (Israel), and is well below $20 million for the selected counties. The minimum offset required as a percentage of contracts is nearly 100 per cent for these counties with few exceptions such as Israel (35%) and Taiwan (70%) that demand less. The relatively advanced industrialised countries such as the UK and Italy prefer only defence-related offsets and the European countries, on an average prefer nearly 75 per cent direct-related offsets and the rest are civil indirect offset. Beside, countries also use other methods as a part of their offset policy.

The Defence offset policy of select countries is tabulated as shown below:-

Defence Offset Policy of Selected Countries

AUSTRALIA	
Title Policy	Australia Industry Involvement (All) Programme
Agency Handling	Department of Defence, Defence Material Organization
Part of Procurement Decision	Yes, for military procurement
Offset Sector	Defence
Minimum Value of Contract	Civilian–A$10 million (US $7.5 million); Defence–A$5 million (US $3.75 million)
Minimum Offset Required	No Specific Min. or Max.
Term	7 years unless otherwise defined in agreement
Multipliers	None in policy
Penalties	Penalties negotiated in each agreement, but generally more than 10% of contract value
Focus	Long-term partnerships with an emphasis on operational requirements, life support systems and research and development–all defence-related
Direct vs. Indirect	Both
Eligible Offset Activities	Subcontract, R&D, technology transfer, training and skills transfer, export sales, infrastructure, venture capital

CANADA	
Title of Policy:	Industrial & Regional Benefits Policy (IRB)
Agency Handling	Industry Canada under the Ministry of Industry
Part of Procurement Decision	Yes
Offset Sector	Civilian and Defence
Minimum Value of Contract	Discretionary for contracts over C$2million (US$1.7 million); C$100m required (US $84 million)
Minimum Offset Required	100%
Term	From release of Letter of Interest or RFP to the end of the export contract
Multipliers	None in policy
Penalties	Liquidated damages are applied for non-compliance
Focus	Investment in the high-tech sectors of the economy
Direct vs. Indirect	Both
Eligible Offset Activities	Investment, technology transfer, co-production,R&D, Both major and non-major Crown projects

FINLAND	
Title of Policy:	Policy on Industrial Participation
Agency Handling	Finnish Committee on Industrial Participation, Ministry of Trade and Industry
Part of Procurement Decision	Yes
Offset Sector	Defence
Minimum Value of Contract	10 • million
Minimum Offset Required	100%
Term	To be negotiated
Multipliers	0.3-3 for exports of Finnish products; technology transfer, and marketing assistance multipliers are negotiated
Penalties	3-5%, exclusion from future procurements
Focus	Participation of domestic defence industry,technology, export, internationalization of exports
Direct vs. Indirect	Both
Eligible Offset Activities	Subcontract, exports and internationalization of SMEs, technology transfer, co-production, marketing assistance

GREECE	
Title of Policy:	Policy of Offsets Benefits (OB)
Agency Handling	Hellenic Ministry of National Defence/General Armaments Directorate (GAD), Division of Offsets (DO)
Part of Procurement Decision	Yes
Offset Sector	Defence
Minimum Value of Contract	10 • million
Minimum Offset Required	100% (often exceeds this, average is understood to be around 120%)
Term	Same as period of procurement contract
Multipliers	Very complex, depends on value of offset and recipient, up to 10
Penalties	10% of unfulfilled benefits, 1.5% penalty late fee per month
Focus	Upgrade production and technology infrastructure, reinforce armed forces, reduce procurement costs
Direct vs. Indirect	Both
Eligible Offset Activities	Required: local subcontracting, purchase and/or coproduction; Other options: direct investment, material/services to armed forces directly, others defined in specific agreement (training and technical support do not count)

ISRAEL	
Title of Policy:	Industrial Cooperation (Industrial Cooperation Program – ICP)
Agency Handling	Industrial Cooperation Authority (ICA), Ministry of Trade and Industry
Part of Procurement Decision	Yes (Mandatory Tenders Law Regulations require ICP)
Offset Sector	Civilian (Under GPA) and Defence
Minimum Value of Contract	US $500,000
Minimum Offset Required	35%
Term	Length of time of the contract, may be extended
Multipliers	1-1.5 times, dependent upon type of offset
Penalties	No liquidated damages clause
Focus	Development of close, long-term working relationships
Direct vs. Indirect	Both
Eligible Offset Activities	Subcontract (preferred), purchase, direct investment, R&D

ITALY	
Title of Policy:	Not codified
Agency Handling	National Armament Directorate, Ministry of Defence
Part of Procurement Decision	Armed Services
Offset Sector	Defence
Minimum Value of Contract	5• million (about $6.6m) unless the seller's country has obligations with the Italian industry
Minimum Offset Required	100% target, but no less than 70%
Term	-
Multipliers	Negotiable, maximum of 3
Penalties	Maximum penalty of 10%
Focus	Provide export opportunities for Italian defence companies
Direct vs. Indirect	Both
Eligible Offset Activities	Export of Italian military products

NETHERLANDS	
Title of Policy:	Industrial Benefits and Offsets Policy
Agency Handling	Ministry of Economic Affairs – Commissariat for Military Production (CMP)
Part of Procurement Decision	Yes
Offset Sector	Civilian and Defence
Minimum Value of Contract	5• million
Minimum Offset Required	100%
Term	Generally 5-7 years from date of agreement is in effect, but not to exceed 10
Multipliers	Negotiable, ranges of 1-5, 5-10, and 10-30
Penalties	15% or 30%, must still fulfil obligation
Focus	Technological innovation, marketing support for innovative products
Direct vs. Indirect	Both
Eligible Offset Activities	Co-production, licensed production, technology transfer, R&D, investment, marketing assistance.

NORWAY	
Title of Policy:	Guidelines for the Establishment and Implementation of Offsets in Connection With Defence Procurements
Agency Handling	Ministry of Economic Affairs – Commissariat for Military Production (CMP)
Part of Procurement Decision	Yes
Offset Sector	Civilian and Defence
Minimum Value of Contract	50 NoK ($6.7 million)
Minimum Offset Required	100%
Term	Length of Contract
Multipliers	0-5
Penalties	15% or 30%, must still fulfill obligation
Focus	Strengthen and maintaining the technical capability of Norwegian Defence industry
Direct vs. Indirect	Both (Indirect preferred)
Eligible Offset Activities	Technology transfer, investment, co-production, R&D

POLAND	
Title of Policy:	Polish Act on Offset Programs
Agency Handling	Committee for Offset Agreements, Ministry of Economy
Part of Procurement Decision	Yes
Offset Sector	Civilian and Defence
Minimum Value of Contract	5• million
Minimum Offset Required	100% (direct must account for 50%)
Term	Minimum of 36 Months, Max 10 years
Multipliers	0.5-2% (Negotiable up to 2-5%)
Penalties	Pay additional multiplier or credit value of commitment
Focus	Technological innovation, marketing support for innovative products
Direct vs. Indirect	Both
Eligible Offset Activities	Technology transfer, investment, co-production, or other agreed upon activities (pending approval)

SOUTH KOREA	
Title of Policy:	Korean Defence Offset Program
Agency Handling	Defence Acquisition Program Administration, Defence Procurement Agency, MND-Korea
Part of Procurement Decision	Yes
Offset Sector	Defence
Minimum Value of Contract	$10 million
Minimum Offset Required	30%
Term	Usually Contract length
Multipliers	Determined by MND
Penalties	Per case but usually 10%
Focus	Defence
Direct vs. Indirect	Both
Eligible Offset Activities	Technology transfer, co-production, R&D, and other flexible activities

Chapter – 4

India's Defence Offset Policy

Introduction

India's offset policy was articulated for the first time in the Defence Procurement Procedure 2005 (DPP 2005). The policy of 2005 was further elaborated in DPP 2006 and subsequently revised under DPP 2008. The offset policy as enunciated in DPP 2008 mandates a minimum 30 per cent offsets in all capital acquisitions (except those under fast track procedure) which are worth three billion rupees or more.

Scope of India's Defence Offset Policy

As per DPP provision, offset would apply to all capital acquisitions whose estimated value is Rs. 300 crore or above and are categorized as 'Buy (Global)' (i.e., outright purchase from foreign/Indian vendors) and 'Buy and Make with Transfer of Technology' (i.e., purchase from foreign vendor followed by licensed production). In case of 'Buy and Make with Transfer of Technology', offsets (of minimum 30 per cent) would be applicable on the foreign exchange component.

The DAC has the freedom to either waive off or prescribe higher offsets exceeding 30 per cent, depending upon the factors such as type of acquisition, strategic importance of the acquisition or technology, enhanced ability of Indian defence industry to absorb the offset, export potential generated, etc. The offset conditions are part of the RFP, the final contract and are binding.

Discharge of Offset Obligations

As per the DPP provisions, the offset obligations of the foreign vendors can be discharged through any combinations of the following methods:

- Direct purchase of, or executing export orders for, eligible products and components manufactured by, or services provided by, Indian industries, i.e. Defence Public Sector Undertakings, the Ordnance Factory Board and private Indian industry. A list of products eligible for discharge of offsets is given in Annexure-2.
- Direct foreign investment in Indian industries for industrial infrastructure for services, co-development, joint ventures and co-production of eligible products and components.
- For the purpose of discharge of offsets, 'services' will mean maintenance, overhaul, upgradation, life extension, engineering, design, testing of eligible products and related software or quality assurance services with reference to eligible products as indicated in Annexure-2 and training. Training may include training services and training equipment (e.g. simulators) but exclude civil infrastructure.
- Direct foreign investment in Indian organisations engaged in research in defence research and development (R&D) as certified by Defence Offset Facilitation Agency. While certifying, DOFA shall not consider civil infrastructure and such technologies that are otherwise easily available in the open market.
- Foreign vendors could consider creation of offset programmes in anticipation of future obligations. Offset credits so acquired can be banked and discharged against future contracts. Banked offset credits would not be transferable except between the main contractor and his sub-contractors within the same acquisition programme. The main contractor would be required to submit a list of such subcontractors at the time of signing the contracts.

Banking of Offset Credit

The DPP-2008 introduced Banking of Offset Credit, which came into effect from September 01, 2008. Under the banking provision, foreign vendors are allowed to accumulate credits for discharging their future offset obligations. The provision allows two ways for accumulation: one, through prior investment in the Indian defence sector; and, two, by generating excess credits from the ongoing offset projects. In other words, the banking provision allows foreign vendors prior as well as continuous opportunities in Indian defence industry, to discharge their future offset obligations.

Conditions/Requirements under Banking of Offset Credit

- A vendor is allowed to discharge his banked offset credit for the RFPs.
- The banked offset credits are non-transferable except between the main contractor and his sub-contractors within the same acquisition programme.
- The validity of the approved banked offset credits is limited to maximum two-and-a-half years. For calculation of validity period, the cut off dates would be 1st April and 1st October of the financial year. As an illustration, offset credits which have been approved and banked on or after 1st April 2010 would be valid for discharge against RFPs issues up to 30th September 2012. Similarly, offset credits on or after 1st October 2010 would be valid for discharge against new RFPs issued up to March 2013.
- If a vendor generates more offsets than his obligations under a particular contract, the surplus offset credits can be banked. They would remain valid for the period of two financial years after conclusion of the said contract. The surplus offset credits can be used for discharging against the new RFPs which would be floated within this period.

- Wherever the offset banking/discharge is done by way of investment in Indian defence industry, including in R&D sector, the related foreign investment should remain valid and active throughout the duration of the MoD contract in relation to the RFP.
- The vendor will submit in a prescribed format reports on implementation of banked offset credits to the Offset Monitoring Cell every six months. The vendor will inform Offset Monitoring Cell about the RFP against which he wants to discharge the banked credits. The details of the banked credits would be transferred to the respective Acquisition Managers after the RFP is issued.

Multiplier

As of now, there is no provision for multiplier under India's Defence offset policy.

Defence Offset Facilitation Agency (DOFA)

To facilitate implementation of offset policy, a 'single-window' agency – the DOFA – has been set up within the MoD's Department of Defence (DDP) consisting of representatives from three service headquarters, Headquarters Integrated Defence Staff (HQ IDS), Defence Public Sector Undertakings (DPSUs), Ordnance Factories (OFs), the Defence Research and Development Organisation (DRDO), and industry associations. The agency, headed by a Joint Secretary, is a multidisciplinary body tasked to perform the following functions:

a) Facilitate implementation of the offsets policy

b) Assist potential vendors in interfacing with the Indian defence industry

c) Assist in vetting offset proposals technically

d) Assist in monitoring the offset provisions

e) Suggest improvements in the policy and procedures

f) Interact with Headquarters Integrated Defence staff and Service Headquarters

g) Advise, in consultation with the Headquarters Integrated Defence staff, Services and Defence Research and Development Organisation, areas in which offsets will be preferred

h) Promote exports of defence products and services.

Partnering Indian Vendors for discharge of Offset Obligations

A foreign vendor has complete freedom to choose its Indian partner for discharging offsets. The foreign vendor has also freedom to change its approved Indian partner mid-way while discharging obligations under some exceptional circumstances. However, for changing Indian partner mid-way, the foreign vendor has to obtain approval from the MoD which would be given only in 'exceptional cases'. The offset component and value as signed in the original contract would, however, not be subject to change to facilitate both the foreign as well as Indian Companies involved in offset related Industrial work. The DPP provides a product list. (See Annexure II)

Stages Involved

Identification of offset projects

It is the responsibility of the Services Capital Acquisition Plan Categorization Higher Committee (SCAPCHC) to identify projects for application of standard 30 per cent offset. Based on the recommendation of SCAPCHC, the DAC takes a final view. Post DAC decision, offset clause becomes a part of RFP and subsequently of the contact to be signed with the winning vendor. Offset conditions as specified in the RFP are binding.

Solicitation of Offers

The foreign vendor, who is interested to participate in the RFP, is required to submit offset proposals. In order to maintain secrecy of the commercial bid of the main contract, the vendor is required to submit only a written undertaking to the effect that it will meet the offset obligations as laid down in the RFP as per the format given in Annexure III. Two separate offers, one commercial offset offer and the other technical offset offer will be submitted subsequently as per the date specified in the RFP. These two proposals (commercial and technical) are to be submitted together in two separate envelopes to the Technical Manager (TM) of the Acquisition Wing of MoD. The timeframe for submission would be specified in the RFP, which would not be earlier than three months from the date of submission of the main technical and commercial offers pertaining to the main contract.

The foreign vendor is required to provide details with regard to products, services and investments proposals indicating related percentages, proposed Indian partners for offset investment and other relevant information in a prescribed format. Also details of banked offset credit as discharged offset obligations will be indicated by the vendor. It is a prerequisite that the commercial values of the offset proposal are not to be indicated in the technical offset offer.

Technical Evaluation of Offset Offers

The technical offset offers (Annexure-IV) so submitted by vendor (s) are to be scrutinized by a Committee constituted by the concerned Technical Manager (TM) with approval from the DG (Acquisition). The Committee consists of representatives from the Armed Forces, Defence Finance, and DRDO. DOFA assists the Committee by providing relevant information as to the technical feasibility of the offset offers. The Committee will examine the compliance of the technical offset offers by the vendor for meeting the offset obligations. The concerned TM forwards the report of the Committee to the DG (Acq) for approval.

While submitting technical offset offers, the vendors need to factor in the following:

- Only contracts for export of defence products or services or investment made after signing of the main contract are reckoned for discharging offset obligations. However, pre-approved offset banking agreements and banked offset credits are considered for discharging of offset obligations. For products which contain imported components, only the value addition in India will count towards offset obligations. In other words, the value of imported components will not count towards offset obligations.

- Offsets will not be applicable for procurements under 'Buy (Global)' if it involves a JV between an Indian company and a foreign company and the indigenous component is at least 50 per cent. If the indigenous content is less then 50 per cent, then the offset will be applicable on the foreign exchange component of the contracted value.

Commercial Offset Offers

Vendors are required to submit their Commercial Offset Offer in a prescribed format (see Annexure V). The Commercial Offset Offer will contain the detailed offer specifying the absolute amount of the offset with a break up of the details, phasing, India partner, and banked credits as discharged obligations. The model format which the vendor is required to fill in the information, may be amended, without deviating from the mandatory offset requirements prescribed.

Examination of Offset Offers

Post submission of Offset Offers (both technical and commercial), are examined in two stages by the Acquisition Wing of the MoD. A committee constituted by the concerned Technical Manager will first examine all Technical Offset Offers, keeping in view that the offset offers submitted by vendors comply with the mandatory requirements. Those vendors whose technical offers comply with the mandatory requirements as specified in the RFP qualify for opening of Commercial Offset Offers.

The Commercial Offset Offers are opened along with the main commercial offers of those vendors who qualify in the stage of Technical Evaluation/Field Trials. The CNC while determining the L1 Vendor also ensures that Commercial Offset Offers submitted by the vendors meet the offset obligations as stipulated in the RFP. The L1 vendor is allowed to amend its commercial Offset Offer at the CNC stage, to meet the minimum offset requirement as prescribed in the RFP.

It is noteworthy that the Commercial Offset Offer does not have any bearing on the determination of L1 vendor. If the L1 vendor's submitted Commercial Offset Offer does not meet the minimum offset requirement as prescribed in the RFP, the vendor is allowed to make amends to meet the minimum offset requirement. Once this is ensured, the L1 vendor is invited to sign the main contract and the offset contract.

Offset Contract

The offset contract is signed with the main contract (see Annexure VI for model Offset Contract). Once signed, the vendor is not permitted to delay the main contract on the pretext of problems in executing offset contract. The various stages as discussed above are shown in the diagram alongside for easy comprehension.

Monitoring Implementation of the Offset Contract

Post-signing of offset contract, the vendor is required to submit quarterly report in a prescribed format (see Annexure VII) to the concerned Acquisition Manager on status of implementation of offset contract. The Offset Monitoring Cell in the MoD assists the concerned Acquisition Manager in monitoring the progress of implementation of offset contract. Further audit by a nominated official or agency is also a possibility to ascertain the actual status of implementation.

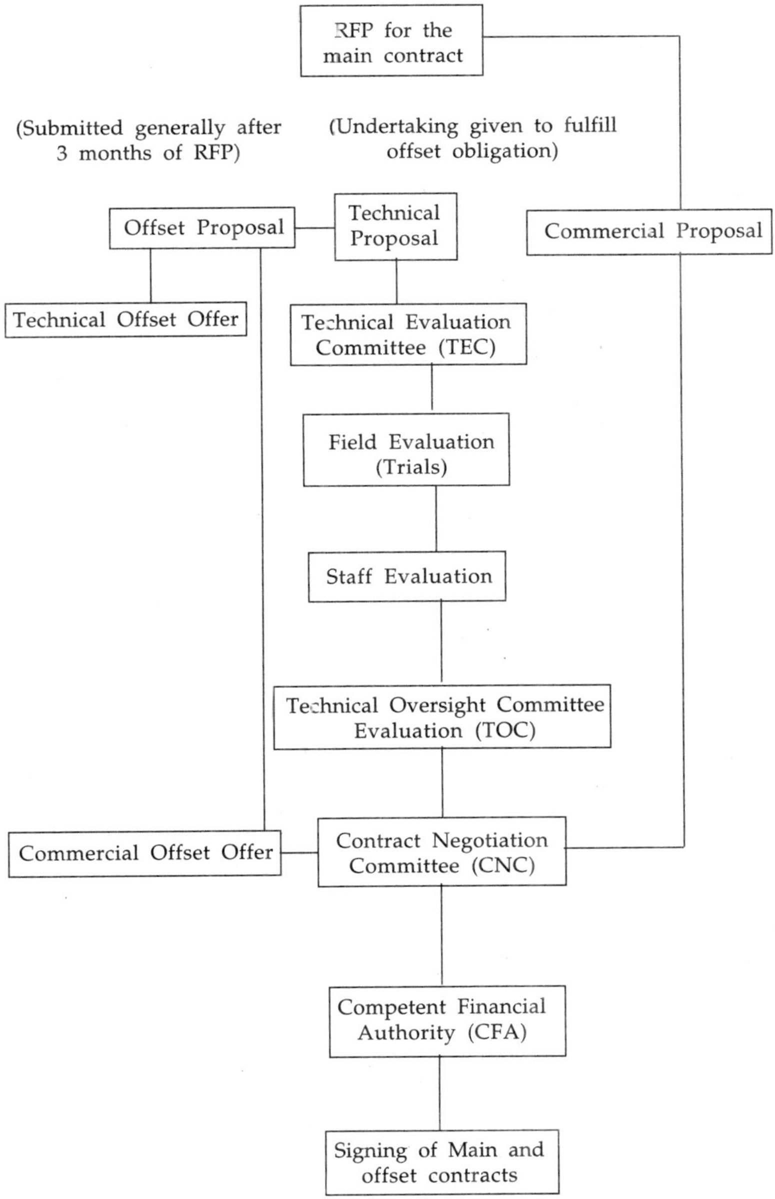
RFP for the main contract
(Submitted generally after 3 months of RFP)
(Undertaking given to fulfill offset obligation)
Offset Proposal
Technical Proposal
Commercial Proposal
Technical Offset Offer
Technical Evaluation Committee (TEC)
Field Evaluation (Trials)
Staff Evaluation
Technical Oversight Committee Evaluation (TOC)
Commercial Offset Offer
Contract Negotiation Committee (CNC)
Competent Financial Authority (CFA)
Signing of Main and offset contracts

Conditions and other applicable rules under Offset Policy

- The offset obligations of a foreign vendor are to be fulfilled within the period of main contract.
- All offset offers which meet the minimum conditions will be treated equally and no extra preferences are allowed for providing offsets more than minimum prescribed.
- A vendor may, giving reasons, request re-phasing of the offset obligations within the period of the main contract. Director General (Acquisition) may allow the request in consultation with DOFA if the reasons submitted are found reasonable and justified.
- Any request on exceptional grounds for extension of the period of the offset contract beyond the period of the main contract is to be examined by the Acquisition Wing in consultation with DOFA and placed before the Defence Acquisitions Council for decision.
- If a vendor fails to fulfil the offset obligation in a particular year, a penalty equivalent to the unperformed offset obligation will be levied, at the rate of 5% of the value of the unfulfilled portion of the annual offset obligation. This will be paid as penalty or recovered from the bank guarantee of the main contract, subject to replenishment, or deducted from the amount payable under the main contract, and the unfulfilled offset value will be carried forward to the subsequent year.
- Any vendor failing to implement the full offset obligations during the period of the main contract, or during the period duly extended, will be liable to be disqualified for participation in future defence contracts. The disqualification will be decided by the Acquisition Wing after giving an opportunity to the vendor to explain the reasons.
- Any differences or disputes will be settled through discussions. The decision of the Acquisition Wing will be final. The provisions in the main contract regarding arbitration will apply to the offset contract also.

Chapter – 5

India's Defence Offset Policy : Prospects and Concerns

Since the detailed promulgation of policy in 2006, the Ministry of Defence has signed around 10 offset agreements with overseas companies which include Rosoboronexport (Russia), RAC MiG (Russia), Fincantieri (Italy), Lockheed Martin (USA), Boeing (USA), Elta (Israel), Israel Aerospace Industries (Israel) and Rafael (Israel). The estimated value of the offsets involved in these contracts is over Rs. 8909 crores. The benefits of offsets will accrue to both Defence Public Sector Undertakings as well as to private Indian Industry engaged in the manufacture of defence systems and equipments. In private sector, 31 companies have so far been benefitted.

India's defence budget is on an increasing trend, reaching US$ 32.1 billion in 2010-11. By 2014-15, it is expected to touch US $42 billion, including US $ 19.4 billion under capital expender, most of which is spent on capital acquisition. The cumulative expenditure on capital acquisition between 2010 and 2015 is expected to be around US$ 65 billion.

India's Defence Budget Projected

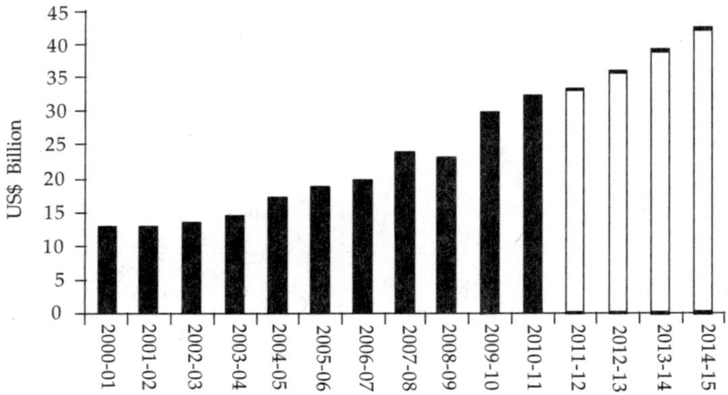

Source: Ministry of Defence and Report of the 13th Finance Commission

The mandatory offset provision in capital acquisition is likely to result in many offset programmes (see Table). In next couple of years as per the sources in the MoD, "there are 41 offset contracts worth more than Rs. 49000 crores in the pipeline at various stages of negotiations which are going to materialise in the near future."

The projects in the pipeline are given below:

Offset Projections

Proposals	Estimated quantity	Cost in US $ (million)	Minimum % of	Offset Value in US$ (Million)
MiG-29 Upgrade	67	677	30%	200
Medium Light Helicopter	172	286	30%	85
Adl. Op. Capability–UAV Sqns	07	71	30%	20
VVIP Helicopter	12	167	30%	50
MMMRCA	126	9333	50%	4650
ASW Helicopter	–	391	30%	120
155 Arti Fd Gun	140	667	30%	30

Contd.

KA 28 Upgrade Short Range Quick Reaction Surface-to-Air Missiles (QRSAM) Advanced MRMR Planes	– 78 6	100 1400 320	30% 30% 30%	30 420 96
Transportable Radars AFV Protection and Counter Measure Systems	– –	1200 270	30% 30%	360 80
Tracked Howitzers EL/M-2083 Aerostat Air-Search Radars	100 9	2000 2700	30% 30%	600 810
Air Defence System	-	1000	30%	333
T-90 EW System	1657	-	-	-
C 130J Hercules	6	1100	30%	300
Naval Multirole Helicopters LCA Engine	16 99	1000 600	30% 30%	300 180
Combat Helicopters Airborne Early Warning and Control Systems	22 145	550 400	30% 30%	165 120
Ultra-light Howitzers Wheeled Howitzers	185 6	667 1000	30% 30%	200 300
Diesel Electric Submarines		6200	30%	1860

Concerns/Limitations

Even though India has succeeded in signing a number of contracts, the objective of enhancing domestic technological and manufacturing capability through offsets does not seem to have progressed in a desired manner. According to high-placed sources, present offset transactions are mostly in the form of outsourcing, and sub-contracting of minor works, which would have taken place in the absence of a formal policy. The offset policy has only succeeded in compelling the foreign companies to place orders with Indian companies without any meaningful enhancement of their capabilities.

The biggest weaknesses of India's offset policy are its open-ended nature, the lack of an effective facilitating/ monitoring/supervising agency, absence of use of innovative methods prevalent in other countries.

Complete Freedom to Foreign OEMs

The policy in the present form provides complete freedom to foreign OEMs to choose any of the three options, as mentioned earlier, for discharging offset obligations. Given this freedom, the foreign companies are expected to choose the easiest option, i.e., exploiting the present strength of the Indian industry. This however defeats the very purpose of enhancing the domestic industrial capability, which requires a quantum jump from the current technological capabilities. For this to happen, the policy needs to guide the offset inflows into the desired areas which are in the country's long term requirements. This requires a comprehensive technological roadmap, formulated in consultations with the Services, and Industry among others, and put to leverage against offsets.

Rigid FDI Policy and differing Perceptions

In a major policy revision the MoD in 2001 opened up its defence industry 100 per cent to the private sector and allowed foreign direct investment (FDI) upto 26 per cent, both subject to licensing. The FDI cap of 26 per cent was however not viewed positively by the foreign vendors, who are reluctant to invest in and part with sensitive technology to an Indian joint venture in which they have little control. This is one reason why nearly nine years after liberalization of Indian defence industry, total FDI inflows is at an abysmally low level. (As per the latest data released by the government, the cumulative FDI inflow into defence industries is US$ 0.15 million - a fraction of investment inflows into sectors like Sugar and Timber Products, among others.)

As FDI is one of the ways that foreign vendor can resort to for discharging offset obligations, there has been a strong pitch by the overseas companies to overcome the rigidity of the FDI cap and raise it to at least 49 per cent. However the government has so far not been able to arrive at a consensus, with key ministries advocating different policy paths. The Ministry of Finance in its broad policy recommendations, as outlined in *Economic Survey 2008-09*, had suggested to increase FDI to 49 per cent, across the board and "up to 100 per cent on a case by case basis, in high technology, strategic defence goods, services and systems that can help eliminate import dependence." The Commerce Ministry believes that Indian Defence industry should be opened up 100 per cent for established foreign companies. Recently, it has reportedly sent a note to the Cabinet Secretariat for discussion in this regard. In contrast, the MoD is of the view that the 49 per cent cap can be considered on a "case-by-case basis", and on the condition that "industry is able to convince us."

The different perceptions among the Ministries apart, the Indian industry, which is the key stakeholder of any revision in FDI policy, does not seem to be in agreement, although majority seem to favour an increase in it to 49 per cent. As a recent joint report by Ernst and Young and Confederation of Indian Industry (CII) brings out, some 58 per cent of the industrial bodies interviewed by them are in favour of raising it to 49 per cent while 17 per cent are in agreement of raising it further.

Notwithstanding the differing perceptions, the fact of the matter is that when FDI was allowed it was not so much for financial considerations as the need for attracting technology into India. Given India's poor track record in defence R&D and near absence of any meaningful military research activity in the private domain in particular, an increase in FDI is the most vital instrument in bringing technology inflow into India.

Non allowance of Multiplier and Transfer of Technology (ToT)

The DPPs of 2006, 2008 and 2011 do not consider multiplier and technology transfer as part of offset transactions, although the same is part of India's overall procurement policy. As regards multipliers, the DPP-2011, for example, clearly states, "all offset offers which satisfy the minimum eligibility conditions will be placed on par and no preference will be given for any extra amount offered." Contrary to the Indian provision, multiplier is a preferred practice followed by many countries. An indication of this is provided by the US Department of Commerce's Bureau of Industry and Security, which submits an annual report to the Congress on the impact of offsets in defence trade. As its latest report shows, over 12 per cent of all offsets transactions incurred by the US companies between 1999 and 2008 involved multipliers of greater than one. Moreover, technology transfer is one of the three most preferred categories which involved multiplier. According to BIS report, during the period 1999-2008, technology transfer accounted for nearly 23 per cent of all offset transactions.

At present the non-provisioning of technology transfer in India's offset scheme is largely driven by the fear that foreign Original Equipment Manufactures (OEMs) would "dump redundant technologies' on Indian industry. The fear, which is prevalent in both the domestic industry as well as the Defence Ministry, is largely due to the absence of an agency which can evaluate the kind of technology required and put a price on it. In addition, the Indian industry opposes multiplier as it reduces the commercial value of a transaction by giving more credit than its calculated value. The fear, however genuine in the current situation, needs to be overcome, considering that technology inflows have the potential of raising the capability bar of Indian industry.

Limited Credit Banking Period

Although the DPP-2011 has allowed offset credit banking, the permissible period for such banking, which at present is two and half years, is too short to attract prior investment. Countries such as Denmark allows five years for banking purposes. The logic behind such longer provision is to allow foreign companies to complete long drawn defence contracts and at the same time accumulate credits for using in future contracts. If a concerned foreign company fails to win a particular contract, there is still hope of utilising those parked credits because of the longer validity period. In India where the objective of offsets is to enhance domestic industrial capability through foreign participation, a short two-and-a-half-years validity period does not provide adequate incentive to overseas companies, to invest in India's long-term defence projects. That is why no single offset credit has so far been banked with or approved by the MoD. These credits are also not transferable except between the main contractor and the sub-contractor within the same acquisition programme.

Weak DOFA

Although DOFA has been created with the purpose of the facilitating potential as well as actual offset transaction between foreign OEMs and Indian industry, the agency however needs to be strengthened with adequate manpower, both in terms of number and the quality, to perform its assigned tasks effectively. (The current manpower of the DOFA comprises of a JS level officer who is supported by few others below his rank, drawn from Services and MoD). Given the fact that DOFA has to facilitate a very large volume of offset-related work – estimated to be worth $10 billion in the 11th Five Year Plan (2007-2012) – the agency needs to be expanded, with a dedicated pool of personnel under its belt to perform various tasks. As the offset related tasks pertains to various aspects falling in the domains of legal, financial and technological, the expansion of DOFA needs to factor these aspects. Besides, as the industry is the key stakeholder of DOFA's decision, an effective mechanism should also be put in place for constant interaction. Under the new guidelines issued vide the current DPP, DOFA has not been assigned any specific role in assisting the acquisition manager for monitoring and implementation of offsets. This responsibility has been given to the offset monitoring cell in the Ministry of Defence. On the other hand, DOFA has been given the responsibility in assisting the Acquisition wing in the rephasing of the offset obligations within and outside the period of the main contract under the normal conditions and also in rephasing offset obligations under exceptional and force majeure conditions. This places DOFA in a piquant situation as they are expected to perform the role as defined by the new guidelines without actually getting involved in regular monitoring of the offset contract. This is in direct contravention with the stated objectives of DOFA which includes facilitating the function of industrial alliances and improving the administration of all offset contracts.

Tax Regime

In India, taxes of various forms are levied by Central government, state governments and also the local bodies. The Central government levies taxes on income, customs duties, central excise and service tax among others. Besides the Central government levies taxes such as surcharge and education cess to meet certain objectives. The state governments are authorized to levy VAT (Value Added Tax), stamp duty, state excise and land revenue among others. Tax on properties, octroi and utilities tax on water and electricity, etc are levied by the local bodies.

Although, the Indian taxation system has undergone reform, there are certain issues that affect the industry in general and defence business in private sector in particular. The issues are identified as below:

Level Playing Field between DPSUs and Private Sector. The private sector is at a disadvantage, vis-à-vis the public sector, as the former is required to pay customs duty and/ or service tax on account of:

- "Imported equipment or transfer of intellectual property under licensing arrangements for the purpose of ToT, which is common requirement of procurement contract.
- Training service provided to the armed forces for new equipment and machinery.
- Repair and maintenance services."

Broad Functional Capability Requirement of Armed Forces

The spectrum of requirements as per the long term perspective plans of the three arms of the Indian Defence forces have been made public in broader terms. This is in keeping with the promise made by the minister during the last Expo underlying the need for more openness in defence contracts. However, the information falls short of the expectations as it does not indicate specific requirements in terms of numbers but only indicates generalized field of interest. This is, however, a good beginning.

Army

1. Augment and optimise force application capability
2. Individual Protective Equipment for troops
3. Enhance detection and decontamination equipment in quality and quantity
4. Develop Integrated Field Shelters
5. Address Logistic voids and enhance logistic capability
6. Enhance mobilisation capability
7. Enhance C4I2SAR capability
8. Improve night fighting capability
9. Develop IW capability
10. Improve anti-armour, SAM, ASM and SSM capability
11. Develop and introduce the 'Land Warrior' concept
12. An aviation Quick Reaction capability
13. Indigenisation of bridging technology
14. Improve communication to effect manpower savings and derive maximum benefit from the telecom network
15. Improve and develop Wide Area Network and Satellite Communication Network.
16. Enhance battlespace awareness
17. Enhance force protection capability

Navy

18. Sea Control with Carrier centric CBG capability to cover our area of interests
19. Blue Water deployment and Power Projection with appropriate force levels
20. Networked Operations
21. Expeditionary and Amphibious Capability for one Indep Bde Group
22. Coastal Defence including Minesweeping
23. Sea Denial with adequate Sub surface capability including submarine and ASW
24. Maritime Surveillance (Space based and Airborne - Long Range, Medium Range, Short Range)
25. AEW capability (Rotary & fixed wing)
26. Air to Air refuelling
27. Base infrastructure including development of new bases.
28. CI2SR capability – ship based, air based and UAV borne
29. Special operations including covert launch capability
30. Salvage and Deep Diving capability and EOD.
31. Precision strike capability ashore
32. Establish credible submarine rescue capability
33. Enhance hydrographic survey force levels and technology

Air Force

34. Capability to maintain day and night operations in all weather conditions
35. Modernise and upgrade the fleets of aircraft to meet challenges of advancement in technology

36. Develop stand-off weapon capability during day and night
37. Develop Force Multipliers like FRA, AWACS, AEW&C, surface surveillance, UAV, UCAV etc
38. Develop future AD assets in terms of radars and SAGW to address multi-level, multi-mode threats and to operate in networked environment
39. Develop multi-spectrum offensive and defensive IEW capability, including space based capability and operational infrastructure for analysis of data and real time transmission
40. Develop space based assets for C4ISR, communication of all types, navigation, meteorology etc
41. Enhance operation support infrastructure on an incremental basis in conjunction with modernisation/ induction of systems/equipment
42. Capacity building of training infrastructures for larger numbers in steps with the advancement of technology
43. Development and enhancement of indigenous R&D

BROAD TECHNOLOGY REQUIREMENT OF ARMED FORCES

Joint Technology Requirement

1. Artificial Intelligence
2. Mobile computing
3. Nanoscience
4. Bio-metrics
5. Smart structures
6. MEMS
7. Mobile Wireless Communications
8. Compact power sources
9. Surveillance sensors
10. Electronic Warfare

Army

1. Battlefield Transparency
2. Combat Systems
3. Communication Systems
4. Rockets and Missiles Systems
5. Directed Energy Weapons
6. Advanced Material Technology
7. Artificial Intelligence
8. Robotics
9. Nano Technology
10. Bio-technology
11. Non Lethal Weapons
12. Combat Modeling and Simulation
13. Nuclear, Biological and Chemical Warfare Defence

Navy

1. Marine Engineering
2. Electrical Engineering
3. Weapons and Sensors
4. Submarine Equipment and Systems
5. Project – 75 Equipment and Systems

Air Force

1. Replacement/modernisation of combat aircraft, transport aircraft, helicopters and training aircraft
2. Induction of Force Multipliers
3. Acquisition of modern armament and weapon systems
4. Strengthening of Air Defence Networks/systems/weapons
5. Building up of Information and Electronic Warfare capability

6. Setting up of reliable and secure communication facilities
7. Space based systems and their exploitation
8. Integrated Air Operations Command & Control System (IACCS)
9. Modernisation of training facilities
10. Development of operational infrastructure

These functional capability requirements will ultimately get replicated as firm proposals for acquisition in the times to come. This list will help the perspective sellers to prepare themselves well in advance for the future requirements of the Indian Armed forces and also will help them in planning their offset obligation partners well in advance to give them leading edge at the time that the actual acquisition process starts.

Annexures

ANNEXURE – I

BROAD TIMEFRAME FOR DEFENCE CAPITAL ACQUISITION ACTIVITIES

Sr No.	Stage of Procurement	Time (in weeks)	Cumulative Time (in weeks)	Offset Activity	Time (in Weeks)	Cumulative Time (in weeks)
1.	Acceptance of Necessity					
2.	Initiation of draft REF for collegiate vetting at MoD	04	04	-	04	04
3.	Issue of RFP	04	08	-	04	08
4.	Pre Bid Meeting	06	14	-	-	-
5.	Dispatch of Pre Bid reply	03	17	-	-	-
6.	Receipt of Responses	03	20	Receipt of Offset Compliance Commitment	12	20
7.	Completion of TEC Report	12	32	Submission of Technical and Commercial Offset Proposals	12	32
8.	Acceptance of TEC Report	04	36	Acceptance of TOEC report by DG (Acq)	8-12	40-44
9.	Completion of Technical Offset Evaluation Committee Report	04-08 (concurrent activity)	36 (concurrent activity)	-	-	-
10.	Acceptance of Technical Offset Evaluation Committee Report	04 (concurrent activity)	36 (concurrent activity)	-	-	-
11.	Completion of Field Evaluation (Trials)	20-45	56-81	-	-	-
12.	Completion of Staff Evaluation	04	60-85	-	-	-
13.	Acceptance of Trials/Staff Evaluation Report	04	64-89	-	-	-

Sr No.	Stage of Procurement	Time (in weeks)	Cumulative Time (in weeks)	Offset Activity	Time (in Week)	Cumulative Time (in weeks)
14.	Acceptance of TOC Report (If applicable)	04	68-93	-	-	-
15.	(i) Finalisation of CNC Report (ii) Finalisation of Offset Contract	(i) Multi vendor-06 (ii) Resultant Single Vendor 18-26	(i) Multivendor 74-99 (ii) Resultant Single Vendor 86-119	Evaluation of Commercial Offset Offers will be done concurrently by CNC	Concurrent with other negotiations	74-137
16.	Obtaining of CFA-MoD/MoF CCS approval	04-16	(i) Multivendor 78-115 (ii) Resultant Single Vendor 90-135			
17.	Signing of Main Contract & Signing of Offset Contract	02	(i) Multi-vendor (ii) Resultant Single Vendor 92-137			

ANNEXURE – 2

LIST OF DEFENCE PRODUCTS

- Small arms, mortars, cannons, guns, howitzers, anti-tank weapons and their ammunition including fuze.
- Bombs, torpedoes, rockets, missiles, other explosive devices and charges, related equipment and accessories specially designed for military use, equipment specially designed for handling, control, operation, jamming and detection.
- Energetic materials, explosives, propellants and pyrotechnics.
- Tracked and wheeled armoured vehicles, vehicles with ballistic protection designed for military applications, armoured or protective equipment.
- Vessels of war, special naval system, equipment and accessories.
- Aircraft, unmanned airborne vehicles, aero engines and aircraft equipment, related equipment specially designed or modified for military use, parachutes and related equipment.
- Electronics and communication equipment specially designed for military use such as electronic counter-measure and counter counter-measure equipment surveillance and monitoring, data processing and signaling, guidance and navigation equipment, imaging equipment and night vision devices, sensors.
- Specialized equipment for military training or for simulating military scenarios, specially designed simulators for use of armaments and trainers.

- Forgings, castings and other unfinished products which are specially designed for products for military applications and troop comfort equipment.
- Miscellaneous equipment and materials designed for military applications, specially designed environmental test facilities and equipment for the certification, qualification, testing or production of the above products.
- Software specially designed or modified for the development, production or use of above items. This includes software specially designed for modeling, simulation or evaluation of military weapon systems, modeling or simulating military operation scenarios and Command, Communications, Control, Computer and Intelligence (C^4I) applications.
- High velocity kinetic energy weapon systems and related equipment.
- Direct energy weapon systems, related or countermeasure equipment, super conductive equipment and specially designed components and accessories.

Products for Internal Security

- Arms and their ammunition including all types of close quarter weapons.
- Protective Equipment for Security personnel including body armour and helmets.
- Vehicles for internal security purposes including armoured vehicles, bullet proof vehicles and mine protected vehicles.
- Riot control equipment and protective as well as riot control vehicles.
- Specialized equipment for surveillance including hand held devices and unmanned aerial vehicles.
- Equipment and devices for night fighting capability including night vision devices.

- Navigational and communications equipment including for secure communications.
- Specialized counter terrorism equipment and gear, assault platforms, detection devices, breaching gear, etc.
- Training aids including simulators and simulation equipment.

Civil Aerospace Products

- All types of fixed wing as well as rotary aircraft including their air frames, aero engines, aircraft components and avionics.
- Aircraft design and engineering services.
- Technical publications
- Raw material and semi-finished goods.
- Flying training institutions and technical training institutions (excluding civil infrastructure).

SPEARFISH

ANNEXURE – 3

UNDERTAKING TO COMPLY WITH OFFSET REQUIREMENTS

The Bidder ________ (name of the company) hereby

1. Undertakes to fulfill the offset obligation as laid down in the Request for Proposals (RFP).
2. Undertakes to ensure timely adherence to fulfillment of offset obligations
3. Accepts that any failure on the part of the Company to meet offset obligations will render disqualification from any further participation in the contract and render bid offer as null and void.
4. Undertakes to furnish technical details of offset obligations indicating products and services and corresponding Indian Industry partner(s) for the same when so required to by Ministry of Defence, Government of India, after being found to satisfy the SQRs.
5. Undertakes to translate the detailed technical offset offer given at para (4) above into a business implementation plan now furnishing complete commercial details of investments, products and services, Indian Industry partners, amount, phases and time plan for the same in the form of a commercial offset offer as and when so required by MOD, GOI.

ANNEXURE – 4

TECHNICAL OFFSET OFFER

1. The Bidder ________ (name of the company) hereby offers the following Direct Foreign Investment (DFI), products and services with Indian Industry partners in compliance to the technical offset obligations in the RFP.
2. The Bidder hereby also furnishes MoU with Indian Industry partners for the proposed investments, products and services.

OFFER LIST OF PRODUCTS AND SERVICES

S.No.	DFI, Products & Services	Indian Offset Partner	Percentage Cost of Offset	MoU (If Applicable) Obligation	Remarks
1	DFI/Products/ SERVICES	Indian Offset Partner 1	Percentage	Memorandum1	
2	DFI/Products/ SERVICES	Indian Offset Partner 2	Percentage	Memorandum2	
3	Similarly for all				

3. Banked Offset Credits. The bidder will also mention the details of the banked offset credits indicating the Project Identification Number. The bidder will also inform Offset Monitoring Cell in the MoD about this commitment.

Note: The vendor may like to amend the model format given in this Annexure without deviating from the mandatory offset requirements as prescribed in the RFP.

ANNEXURE – 5

COMMERCIAL OFFSET OFFER

1. In compliance with the offset obligations, the Bidder _____ hereby offers following products and services to Indian Industry partners.
2. The Bidder hereby also furnishes MoU(s) with Indian offset partners for applicable investments, products and services.

OFFER LIST OF PRODUCTS AND SERVICES

S.No.	DFI, Products & Services	Indian Offset Partner	Value (with timeframe break up)	Timeframe (Break up)	Remarks
1	DFI/Products/ SERVICES	Indian Offset Partner 1	Percentage	Memorandum1	
2	DFI/Products/ SERVICES	Indian Offset Partner 2	Percentage	Memorandum2	
3	Similarly for all				

3. Details of Foreign Direct Investment/Joint Venture/ Co Development/ToT-Give details
4. Any other contracts with anyone in India - Give details
5. Banked Offset Credits: The bidder will also mention the details of the banked offset credits indicating the Project Identification Number. The bidder will also

inform Offset Monitoring Cell in the MoD about this commitment.

Note: This Annexure is also to be used by the vendor to submit proposals for banking of offsets. In banking of offsets, vendors are not required to fill para 5 of this Annexure.

The vendor may like to amend the model format given in this Annexure without deviating from the mandatory offset requirements as prescribed in RFP.

Annexure – 6

OFFSET CONTRACT

Contract No. ____ **Dated** ____

This Offset Contract enters into this date of __________hereinafter refers to as "Effective Date", is by and between

(a) The President of India represented by the Joint Secretary and Acquisition Manager (Land/Air/Maritime systems, as the case may be) Ministry of Defence, Government of India, New Delhi, hereinafter referred to as the Buyer on one part and

(b) M/s (Name of the Vendor) duly represented by ____________ and incorporated under the laws of ____________ having its registered office at ______ hereinafter referred to as "Seller" on the other part.

Whereas, the Seller has been awarded a Contract, Contract Number ________ dated ______ for the Project entitled,_______________, as the Supply Contract stipulates a total amount of ____________to be paid by the Buyer for the provision of the seller's goods and/or services and

The Buyer clearly understands and agrees to the Offset Clause given in the RFP and the offset schedule defined in the Defence Procurement Procedure 2008 and the offset policy promulgated by the Government of India, referred to as the 'Offset Policy'.

Now, therefore, the Buyer and the Seller agree as follows:

1. The Seller understands and agrees that supply contract is subject to fulfillment of the offset contract/contracts that the seller will execute with the Indian offset partner/ partners towards the complete fulfillment of Offset Obligations laid down in the RFP. The total amount this Offset Obligation is ____________ which is (specified) percent (# %) of the supply contract value.
2. In the event that the supply contract value is increased or reduced then the Seller's Offset Obligations shall be adjusted proportionately.
3. The Offset start date applicable to the Offset Obligations hereunder shall be the effective date of contract number _________.
4. Furthermore, the Seller agrees and promises to perform its Offset Obligation in accordance with the Offset Schedule of the commercial offset offer. The Offset Schedule may not be changed or amended in any way without the prior written agreement of the MoD, Government of India.
5. Within ninety (90) calendar days from the Effective Date of this agreement, the Seller shall, in writing, provide the Ministry of Defence with a copy of the offset programme contracts entered into with the Indian offset partners and a list of the Company's Official Contracts for all matters related to this agreement and the performance of the Seller's Offset Obligation. The list shall specify the name, mailing address, street address, telephone, and facsimile numbers of each Official Contact and shall be limited to three (3) Official Contacts. Any and all communications and correspondence by the Ministry of Defence to any one (1) of the said Official Contacts shall be deemed as if by the Ministry of Defence to the Seller.
6. In the event of force majeure, representative of the MoD and the Seller's official representative will meet

to assess progress to date under the Programme prior to the date of the force majeure event and to determine a mutually agreeable manner and schedule for the fulfillment of the Seller's remaining Offset Obligation.

7. This Contract, and any and all matters relating to the fulfillment of the Seller's Offset Obligations and performance under the Programme shall be interpreted and be subject to the Laws of the Republic of India. This contract shall be governed by and interpreted in accordance with the laws of the Republic of India.

8. This Contract shall expire upon fulfillment of the Company's Offset Obligations in accordance with the Contract.

Annexure – 7

QUARTERLY REPORT ON FULFILLING OFFSET OBLIGATIONS

Report for Quarter Ending __________

1. Main contract No. and effective date ____
2. Banking project ID No. (in case of banking) ____
3. Indian offset partner ____
4. Offset contract number (not required in case of banking) ____
5. Product number and name
6. Schedule of offset obligations and fulfillment

No.	FDI/Products/ Services Offered	Value of Offset Committed	Date by which to by fulfilled	Actual value fulfilled by roporting date	Remarks including penalty if any
(1)	(2)	(3)	(4)	(5)	(6)

7. Explanatory notes, if any
8. Supporting enclosures with respect to column 5 above for actual value fulfilled.

ANNEXURE – 8

FORM - FC/IL
SIA

COMPOSITE FORM FOR FOREIGN COLLABORATION AND INDUSTRIAL LICENCE

Please fill up the attached supplementary sheets

Part A: For only FC/Part B: For only IL/Both Part A and Part B for FC+IL

GENERAL INFORMATION

1. Type of Application (Please √ the Appropriate Boxes)

a. Foreign Collaboration (FC)

For Foreign Investment

For Foreign Technology Agreements

b. Industrial Licence (IL)

2. *(For Office Use Only)*

Application No. ☐☐☐☐☐☐☐☐☐☐☐☐

Application Date ☐ ☐ ☐ ☐ ☐☐☐☐

3. Payment Details (***For FC Application No Fee is Payable. For Industrial Licences Rs. 2500, * is Payable)***

Draft No. ______________________

Amount (Rs.)

Draft Date

Drawn on ______________ Payable at ______________

(Name of the Bank)

****Demand Draft should be made in favour of Pay & Accounts Officer, Deptt. of Industrial***

I. Name and Address of the Promoter/Industrial Undertaking **(Indian/foreign)** in full (BLOCK LETTERS) for Correspondence.

Name of the Promoter/Indl ☐☐☐☐☐☐☐☐☐☐☐☐☐☐☐☐☐☐☐☐

Undertaking ☐☐☐☐☐☐☐☐☐☐☐☐☐☐☐☐☐☐☐☐

Postal Address ☐☐☐☐☐☐☐☐☐☐☐☐☐☐☐☐☐☐☐☐

☐☐☐☐☐☐☐☐☐☐☐☐☐☐☐☐☐☐☐☐

Pin Code ☐☐☐☐☐☐ Telephone ☐☐☐☐☐☐☐☐☐☐

Telex ☐☐☐☐☐☐☐☐☐☐☐☐ Fax ☐☐☐☐☐☐☐☐☐☐

Cable ☐☐☐☐☐☐☐☐☐☐☐☐

E-Mail ☐☐☐☐☐☐☐☐☐☐☐☐☐☐☐☐☐☐☐☐

II. Registrar of Companies Registration No. ☐☐☐☐☐☐☐☐☐☐

III. Status of the Promoter/Industrial Undertaking

III (1) Status of the Promoter/Promoter Undertaking

☐ 1. Central Government Undertaking

☐ 2. State Government Undertaking

☐ 3. State Industrial Government Corpn.

☐ 4. Co-operative Undertaking

☐ 5. Joint Sector Undertaking

☐ 6. Private Sector Undertaking

☐ 7. Individual Promoter

☐ 8. Foreign/NRI/OCB Company

☐ 9. Foreign/NRI Individual

III (2) Indicate whether this proposal is for (Please √ the Appropriate Box)

☐ 1. Establisnment of New Undertaking/Setting up a New Company

☐ 2. Effecting Substantial Expansion

☐ 3. Manufacture of New Articles

☐ 4. Amendments in existing Foreign Collaboration Approval

☐ 5. Inducting Foreign / NRI equity in existing Indian Company

III (3) *(a) Does the activity proposed qualify for automatic route?*

(b) If so, the reasons for seeking approval of the FIPB/ PAB?

IV(1) Location of the Factory/Proposed Activities

Address ☐☐☐☐☐☐☐☐☐☐☐☐☐☐☐☐☐☐☐☐

☐☐☐☐☐☐☐☐☐☐☐☐☐☐☐☐☐☐☐☐

District ☐☐☐☐☐☐☐☐☐☐☐☐☐☐☐☐☐☐☐☐

State ☐☐☐☐☐☐☐☐☐☐☐☐☐☐☐☐☐☐☐☐

Pin Code ☐☐☐☐☐☐ Telephone ☐☐☐☐☐☐☐

Fax ☐☐☐☐☐☐☐☐☐☐☐☐

E-Mail ☐☐☐☐☐☐☐☐☐☐☐☐☐☐☐☐☐☐☐☐

IV(2) Please Indicate whether the proposed location is (Please √ the Appropriate Box)

a. Within 25 kms from the periphery of a city having population above one million according to 1991 census

Yes ☐ No ☐

b. If Yes, then whether it is located in an Industrial area/Industrial estate Designated/set up prior to 25.7.91

Yes ☐ No ☐

V(A) EXISTING ACTIVITIES OF THE COMPANY(Here also specify Item codes as per National Industrial Classification of All Economic Activity, (NIC). 1987.

☐☐☐☐☐☐☐☐

V(B). PROPOSED ACTIVITIES OF THE COMPANY

(1) Items of manufacture (including By-product/Co-product) proposed to be undertaken (supplementary sheets may be used if necessary).

(a) Item code (NATIONAL INDUSTRIAL CLASSIFICATION OF ALL ECONOMIC

(b) Item Description

(c) Proposed Annual Capacity

(d) Existing Capacity *(If, applicable)**

(e) Total Capacity after expansion

(f) Unit of capacity

(g) Description of Activities to be undertaken (if no manufacturing is envisaged)

(2) Whether the Item is covered in Schedule I (Reserved for Public Sector), Schedule II (Under Compulsory Licensing) or Schedule III (Reserved for manufacture in the Small Scale Sector) of the Notification No. 477 (E) Dated 25th July, 1991

Schedule I	Schedule II	Schedule III
Yes ☐	Yes ☐	Yes ☐
No. ☐	No. ☐	No. ☐

(3) Briefly indicate process involved in manufacture of the item (s)

V(C) Attach list of Industrial Licence/Registration/LOI/IEM acknowledgements already issued in favour of the applicant so far.

V(D) Whether the Indian Promoter/Company has had a foreign collaboration earlier? If yes, please specify whether for the same or similar or different products/activity. Please also indicate the Approving Authority and date & No. of the Approval Letter.

(E) Whether the foreign/NRI/OCB collaborator has collaborations with any other Individual/Company in India for the same or similar or different products/activities? If so, please furnish/details

Particulars of approval/Industrial Licence under which existing capacity is indicated may be annexed

VI CAPITAL STRUCTURE

(I) Capital Structure of Existing Indian Company (Amount in Rupees) and proposed capital structure (if revision sought)

	Equity	Preference
(a) Authorised		
(b) Subscribed		
(c) Paid-up		

(II) Pattern of share holding in Paid-up Capital (Amount in Rupees)

	Existing Equity	%	Proposed Equity	%
(a) Foreign Holding				
	Preference share		Percentage	

(b) Non-resident Indian Individual holding/OCB holding

	Equity	%	Equity	%
(i) Repatriable				
	Preference share		Percentage	
	Equity	%	Equity	%
(ii) Non-Repatriable				
	Preference share		Percentage	
	Equity	%	Equity	%
(c) Resident Holding				
	Preference share		Percentage	

(d) Total II [a+b(i+ii)+c]

Equity				
Preference				

VII. Proposed Borrowings (In Rupees)

(i) Public Financial Institution

(ii) Public Borrowing

(iii) Other Sources

(iv) ECB

(v) Promoter Contributions

Total Borrowings

VIII. Please indicate in brief:

(i) The background of the Indian Promotors/Company including Proprietors/Promotor/Directors (attach separate sheet, if necessary)

(ii) The background of the Foreign/NRI/OCB Collaborator/Promoter (attach separate sheet, if necessary)

IX. Investment (in Rupees)

	Existing	Proposed
(A) Land		
(B) Building		
(C) Plant & Machinery		
(i) Indigenous		
(ii) Imported		
(a) CIF Value		
(b) Landed Cost		
(iii) Total [(i)+(ii)(b)]		
(D) Working Capital		
(E) Total		

Investment

[A+B+C(iii)]

X. Export commitments/obligation which the applicant is prepared to undertake.

Item Code ☐☐☐☐☐☐☐☐☐☐☐☐

Year	Units(Tonnes/ number/meters/ any other)	Quantity	% age of Production	FOB Value in Rs.
	(1)	(2)	(3)	(4)	(5)
1st	☐☐☐☐	☐☐☐☐☐☐	☐☐☐☐☐☐☐☐	☐☐☐☐	☐☐☐☐
2nd	☐☐☐☐	☐☐☐☐☐☐	☐☐☐☐☐☐☐☐	☐☐☐☐	☐☐☐☐
3rd	☐☐☐☐	☐☐☐☐☐☐	☐☐☐☐☐☐☐☐	☐☐☐☐	☐☐☐☐
4th	☐☐☐☐	☐☐☐☐☐☐	☐☐☐☐☐☐☐☐	☐☐☐☐	☐☐☐☐
5th	☐☐☐☐	☐☐☐☐☐☐	☐☐☐☐☐☐☐☐	☐☐☐☐	☐☐☐☐
Total					

Please Indicate buy back arrangements, if any

XI. Employment (All Figures in Numbers)

	Existing (If applicable)	Proposed	Total
a. Supervisory	☐☐☐☐☐☐	☐☐☐☐☐☐	☐☐☐☐☐☐
b. Non-Supervisory	☐☐☐☐☐☐	☐☐☐☐☐☐	☐☐☐☐☐☐

XII. Expected date of commencement of commercial production

☐☐ ☐☐ ☐☐☐☐

PART: A
[For Foreign Collaboration]

XIII. Foreign Investment

(a) Financial Collaborator

Name ____________________

Address ____________________

Country ____________________

(b) Amount of foreign equity investment

Amount in Rupees	Percentage of paid-up capital	
☐☐☐☐☐☐☐☐☐☐	☐☐	☐☐

XIV. Foreign Technology Agreement

Name ____________________

Address ____________________

____

Country ____________________

(b) Royalty on Sales

Sales	Percentage of Sales	Period	Please tick (√) whichever is applicable
Domestic			Inclusive of taxes
Export			Net of taxes

(c) Nature and quantum of Lumpsum payment

Name of Foreign currency	Amount of Foreign exchange required	No. of Instalment in which Payments will be made	Please tick (√) whichever is applicable
			Inclusive of taxes Net of taxes

(i) Technical know-how fees

(ii) Payment for design/drawing

(iii) Payment for engineering services

(iv) Payment for use of patents, brand names, trade marks and the like

(v) Any other payment (Please specify the purpose)

XV. (I) Total Foreign Exchange in flow during the period of proposed collaboration

(a) Equity

(b) Foreign Exchange earnings based on f.o.b. value of export obligation/commitment

(II) Total Foreign Exchange outgo during the period of collaboration

(i) Import of machinery and equipment

(ii) Import of raw materials and components

(iii) Import of Spares and consumables

(iv) Dividends and Profits (net of taxes) ☐☐☐☐☐☐☐☐☐☐

(v) Lumpsum payments (net of taxes) ☐☐☐☐☐☐☐☐☐☐

(vi) Royalty payments (net of taxes) ☐☐☐☐☐☐☐☐☐☐

(vii) Design and Drawing fee ☐☐☐☐☐☐☐☐☐☐

(viii) Payment of Foreign Technicians ☐☐☐☐☐☐☐☐☐☐

(ix) Payment on training of Indian Technicians abroad ☐☐☐☐☐☐☐☐☐☐

(x) Commission of Export etc. ☐☐☐☐☐☐☐☐☐☐

(xi) Amount of interest to be paid on external commercial borrowing/ deferred payment credit (Specify details) ☐☐☐☐☐☐☐☐☐☐

(xii) Any other payments (Specify details) ☐☐☐☐☐☐☐☐☐☐

TOTAL (i) to (xii)

Net Foreign Exchange Position

XVI. If this application is for extension of existing collaboration agreement or renewal of the already expired collaboration agreement:

(a) Please indicate the period for which the agreement has already run and attach the copy of the previous approval

No. & date of Approval	Date of commencement of agreement	Date of expiry of agreement
☐☐☐☐☐☐☐☐ ☐☐ ☐☐ ☐☐☐☐	☐☐ ☐☐ ☐☐☐☐	☐☐ ☐☐ ☐☐☐☐

(b) Justification for extension of the collaboration agreement with information about the status of absorption, adaptation and development of the technology already achieved.

(c) (i) Whether you have set up any R & D Cell to absorb the know-how and the progress achieved in this regard

Yes ☐ No ☐

(ii) If yes, please indicate the number and date of communication under which recognised by Department of Science and Technology/Department of Scientific and Industrial Research

☐☐☐☐☐ ☐☐☐☐☐☐☐☐

(iii) Expenditure on R&D facility set up (in Rupees) Annual recurring expenditure

Amount of investment in fixed assets

☐☐☐☐☐☐☐☐☐☐

Annual recurring expenditure

☐☐☐☐☐☐☐☐☐☐

(d) Total payment made so far (Net of taxes) (in Rupees)

a) Lumpsum ☐☐☐☐☐☐☐☐☐☐

b) Royalty ☐☐☐☐☐☐☐☐☐☐

c) Other payment ☐☐☐☐☐☐☐☐☐☐

XVII. Please indicate :

(a) The Regional Office of the RBI to whom a copy of the approval is to be endorsed

____

____

(b) The name of the Authorised Dealer of Foreign Exchange concerned through whom the remittance of Technical know-how fees and Royalty will be made.

Name : ________________________________

Address : ________________________________

I/We hereby certify that the above statements are true and correct to the best of my/our knowledge and belief.

(Signature of Applicant) : ____________________

(Name in block letters) : ____________________

(Designation of the signatory): ____________________

Place : ____________________

Date □□ □□ □□□□

PART: B
[For Foreign Collaboration]

XIII. Foreign Investment

a. Capital Goods for the Projects

	(in rupees)	(US $ Thousand)
Imported		
Indigeneous		

b. Raw Materials (including components, intermediates and packing materials) **per annum**

Imported		
Indigeneous		

	ITEM NAME	QUANTITY
1.		

Unit Value

2.

Unit Value

3.

Unit Value

c. Consumables and Spares for CG for the Project **per annum**

Year	(in rupees)	(US $ Thousand)
Imported		
Indigeneous		

DECLARATION

I/We hereby certify that the above statements are true and correct to the best of my/our knowledge and belief.

(Signature of Applicant) : ____________________

(Name in block letters) : ____________________

(Designation of the signatory) : ____________________

Place : ____________________

Date : ____________________

Note for Guidance of Entrepreneurs submitting applications for grant of Industrial Licence/approval for Foreign Investment and Technology Agreements.

(This part contains information for the guidance of entrepreneurs and may be retained by them; it needs not accompany the application)

GENERAL

1. Application is to be submitted to Secretariat for Industrial Assistance, Department of Industrial Policy and Promotion, Ministry of Industry, Udyog Bhawan, New Delhi with nine copies of both the application and forwarding letter.
2. Applicants are required to take care in filling up their application properly and completely.
3. The application form should be duly signed and the designation/authority of the person signing the application should be clearly shown.
4. Only the relevant part of the application form should be used. General information is to be furnished by all applicants. Part 'A' is to be filled by entrepreneurs/ investors applying for grant of approval for foreign collaboration. Part 'B' is to be used for obtaining Letter of Intent/Industrial Licence. Part 'A' and Part 'B' are to be filled in case of composite proposals involving foreign collaboration and industrial licensing.
5. Application involving grant of Industrial Licence shall be accompanied by a crossed Demand Draft for Rs. 2500/- drawn on the State Bank of India, Nirman Bhawan, New Delhi in favour of the "Pay & Accounts Officer, Department of Industrial Development, Ministry of Industry, New Delhi".

1. FOREIGN INVESTMENT

(i) Approval will be given by the Reserve Bank of India for direct foreign investment upto 50/51/74 per cent foreign equity in high priority industries

(Annex III, Annex III Part 'A', Part 'B' and Part 'C'). There shall be no bottlenecks of any kind in this process.

(ii) The import of components, raw materials and intermediate goods, and payment of know-how fees and royalties will be governed by the general policy applicable to other domestic units.

(iii) Other foreign equity proposals, including proposals involving 50/51/74 per cent foreign equity which do not meet the criteria under (i) above, will continue to need prior clearance. Foreign equity proposals need not necessarily be accompanied by foreign technology agreements.

(iv) To provide access to international markets, majority foreign equity holding upto 51 per cent equity will be allowed for trading companies primarily engaged in export activities. While the thrust would be on export activities, such trading houses shall be at par with domestic trading and export house in accordance with the Import-Export Policy.

(v) For increase/induction of foreign equity in the existing company, the request should be supported by a Board Resolution of the Indian Company.

II. FOREIGN TECHNOLOGY AGREEMENTS

(i) Automatic permission will be given by the Regional Offices of the Reserve Bank of India for foreign technology agreements in high priority industries (Annex III, Annex III Part 'A', Part 'B' and Part 'C') upto a lumpsum payment of US $ 2 million, 5 per cent royalty for domestic sales and 8per cent for exports, subject to total payment of 8per cent of sales over a 10 year period from date of agreement or seven years from commencement of production. The prescribed royalty rates are net of taxes and will be calculated according to standard procedures.

(ii) In respect of industries other than those in Annex III, Annex III Part 'A', Part 'B' and Part 'C', automatic permission will be given subject to the same guidelines as above.

(iii) All other proposals will need specific approvals under the general procedures in force.

(iv) No permission will be necessary for hiring of foreign technicians, foreign testing of indigenously developed technologies. Payment may be made from blanket permits or in free foreign exchange according to RBI guidelines.

III. Standard Conditions Attached to Approvals for Foreign Investment Technology Agreement

1. The total non-resident share-holding in the undertaking should not exceed the percentage(s) specified in the approval letter. In case of any change in the amount of foreign/NRI investment, or the paid-up capital, an intimation to this effect may be given to SIA, RBI and the Administrative Ministry, subject to the percentage of foreign/NRI equity share-holding remaining unchanged.

2. (a) The royalty will be calculated on the basis of the net ex-factory sale price of the product, exclusive of excise duties, minus the cost of the standard bought-out components and the landed cost of imported components, irrespective of the source of procurement, including ocean freight, insurance, custom duties, etc. The payment of royalty will be restricted to the licensed capacity plus 25 per cent in excess thereof for such items requiring industrial licence. In case of production in excess of the quantum, prior approval of the Government will have to be obtained regarding the terms of payment of royalty in respect of such excess production.

   (b) The royalty would not be payable beyond the period of the agreement if the orders had not been executed during the period of agreement. However, where the orders themselves took a long time to execute, then the royalty for an order booked during the period of the agreement, but executed after the period of agreement, would be payable only after a Chartered Accountant certifies that the orders in fact have been firmly booked and execution began during the period of agreement, and the technical assistance was available on a continuing basis even after the period of the agreement.

3. The lumpsum shall be paid in three instalments as detailed below, unless otherwise stipulated in the approval letter: First, 1/3rd after the agreement is filed with Reserve Bank of India/Authorised Foreign Exchange Dealer. Second, 1/3rd on delivery of technical documentation. Third and final, 1/3rd on commencement of commercial production, or four years after the agreement is filed with Reserve Bank of India/Authorised Foreign Exchange Dealer, whichever is earlier. The lumpsum can be paid in more than three instalments subject to completion of the activities as specified above.

4. In case the proposed activity is not exempted from the provisions of Industrial (Development & Regulation) Act, 1951 and the Foreign Exchange Regulation Act, 1973 it will be your responsibility to obtain such clearances as may be required under the said Acts.

5. The location of the industrial projects, will be subject to Central or State Environmental laws or regulations including local zoning and land use laws and regulations.

6. Adequate steps shall be taken to the satisfaction of the Government to prevent air, water and solid pollution measures to be installed should conform to the effluent and emission standards prescribed by the State Government in which the factory or the industrial undertaking is located.

7. Items reserved for Small Scale Sector shall not be manufactured without prior approval of the

Government as per the prescribed policy and procedure.

8. Since the maximum equity participation allowed for in Small Scale Units is 24 per cent, the company's proposal for having, foreign equity of more than 24 per cent would be subject to the condition that the company would get itself de-registered as a small scale unit and obtain industrial license or would file Industrial Entrepreneur Memorandum with SIA as per prescribed policy and procedure.

9. For undertaking the export obligation, if any, specified in the approval letter, the requisite guarantee, i.e. legal undertaking/bank guarantee, as may be required, should be furnished according to the detailed instructions issued by the Directorate General of Foreign Trade (E O Cell), Ministry of Commerce (EP Division) and the Administrative Ministry, who may be contacted in the matter.

10. Import of capital equipment, components and raw materials will be allowed as per the import policy prevailing from time to time

11. The approval is valid for a period of two years from the date of issue. Within this period, the collaboration agreement is required to be filed with Reserve Bank of India/ Authorised Foreign Exchange Dealer.

12. The FC agreement shall be subject to Indian laws.

13. Foreign Investment Remittance (FIRC) is required to be sent to the Reginal Office, Reserve Bank of India, immediately on receipt of foreign remittance.

14. All remittances to the foreign collaborator shall be made as per the exchange rates prevailing on the day of remittance.

15. A copy of the collaboration agreement signed by both the parties may be furnished to the following authorities:

(a) Administrative Ministry/Department as mentioned in the Approval to be issued by SIA.

(b) Secretariat for Industrial Assistance, (Foreign Collaboration-II Section) Department of Industrial Policy and Promotion, Udyog Bhawan, New Delhi -110 011.

(c) Department of Scientific and Industrial Research, Technology Bhawan, New Mehrauli Road, New Delhi-110 016.

16. *The outflow of foreign exchange on account of dividend payment will be balanced by export earnings on the following basis :

a) The balancing of dividends would be over a period of 7 years from commencement of production. Balancing will not be required beyond this period.

b) Remittance of dividends should be covered by earnings of the company from export of items covered by foreign collaboration agreements. You are also to cover remittance of dividends from earnings through export of items not covered by the agreement provided they are covered in the list of industries in Annexure III of Statement by export earnings of such items covered in years prior to the payment of dividends or (*Wherever applicable)

IV. Hiring of Foreign Technicians

No permission is necessary for hiring of foreign technicians and no application needs be made to the Government for this purpose irrespective of whether the hiring of foreign technicians is under an approved collaboration agreement or not. As regards release of foreign exchange either against blanket permits or in free foreign exchange, the Reserve Bank of India/Authorised Dealers may be approached, as per RBI guidelines.

V. Deputation of Indian Personnel for Training Abroad

For deputing Indian personnel for training and other purposes abroad, the entrepreneurs may approach only the RBI/Authorised Dealers as per RBI guidelines.

VI. Foreign Testing of Indigenous Raw Materials and Products and Indigenously Development Technology

Entrepreneurs may approach RBI/Authorised Dealers for authorising payments either against blanket permits or in free foreign exchange, as per RBI guidelines.

OFFICES OF DEFENCE MINISTER AND MINISTER OF STATE FOR DEFENCE

NAME	DESIGNATION	TEL NO. (O)	OFFICE ADDRESS
Mr A K Antony	Raksha Mantri (Defence Minister)	23012286 23019030 23015403 (FAX) 23019474 (PH)	104, South Block, New Delhi
Mr Sundram Krishna	Advisor to Ràksha Mantri	23012286 23019030 23015403(Fax)	107, South Block New Delhi
Mr Dheeraj Gupta	Private Secretary to Raksha Mantri	23012286 23019030 23015403 (FAX)	105, South Block, New Delhi
Dr. K.V. Jacob	OSD to Raksha Mantri	23012286 23019030 23015403 (FAX)	106, South Block, New Delhi
Mr M.M. Pallam Raju	Raksha Rajya Mantri (Minister of State for Defence)	23794621 23792128 23016255 (FAX)	108-B, South Block, New Delhi
Mr Anil Kr. Singhal	Private Secretary to Raksha Rajya Mantri	2379462 12379212 823016255 (FAX)	109-A, South Block New Delhi
Mr Y.S.K. Seshu Kumar	OSD to Raksha Rajya Mantri	23794621 23792128 23016255 (FAX)	109-A, South Block New Delhi.

DEPARTMENT OF DEFENCE

NAME	DESIGNATION	TEL NO. (O)	OFFICE ADDRESS
Mr Pradeep Kumar	Defence Secretary	23012380 23010044(FAX)	101, South Block, New Delhi
Mr Radha Krishna Mathur	Addl. Secretary	2301767 823019658(FAX)	199-B, South Block, New Delhi
Mr Shashi Kant Sharma	Director General (Acquisition)	23014219 23794721(FAX)	137, South Block, New Delhi
Mr Ranjan Kumar Ghose	Joint Secretary & Acqusition Manager (Air)	23014944	8-B, South Block, New Delhi.

Mr Subhash Chandra	Joint Secretary. (G/Air)	23011410 23013709(FAX)	108-A, South Block, New Delhi
Mr Ashok Kumar Gupta	Joint Secretary (C&W) & CVO	2301 5444	198-A, South Block, New Delhi
Mr Binoy Kumar	Joint Secretary (Navy/Ordnance)	23014222	198-B, South Block, New Delhi
Ms Smita Nagaraj	Joint Secretary (PIC)	23011752	109-B, South Block, New Delhi
Mr Jatinderbir Singh	Joint Secretary & Acquisition Manager (Land System)	23015952 23014673(FAX)	130-A, South Block, New Delhi
Mr Upamanyu Chatterjee	Joint Secretary (Trg)	23018201 23018232	155, E-Block, New Delhi.
	Joint Secretary (Estt) & Public Grievances	23792043 23013787(FAX)	97, South Block, New Delhi
Ms. Preeti Sudan	Joint Secretary & Acquisition Manager (Maritime Systems)	23016447 23015875	110, South Block, New Delhi
Mr Subhash Sharma	Secretary Border Road Development Board & JS	23793845 23015884(FAX)	418 'B' Wing Sena Bhawan, New Delhi
Mr K.L.Taneja	Adviser (Statistics)	23015040 23793098	219-'B' Wing Sena Bhawan, New Delhi.
Maj. Gen I.S.Chaturvedi	Technical Manager (Land Systems)	23019609	306, North Hutments, Kashmir House, Rajaji Marg, New Delhi
Rear Admiral B.R. Taneja	Technical Manager. (Maritime & Systems)	23793177	Room No 5, 'D-II' Wing Sena Bhawan, New Delhi
AVM J.S. Panesar	Technical Manager (Air)	23012068	Room No 469, Vayu Bhawan, New Delhi

DEFENCE FINANCE

NAME	DESIGNATION	TEL NO.(O)	OFFICE ADDRESS
Ms. Indu Liberhan	Secretary (Defence Finance)	23016654 23016629	139, South Block, New Delhi
Mr. S.Chandrasekaran	Financial Adviser (Acquisition) & Addl. Secretary	23011250 New Delhi	131-B, South Block, New Delhi
Mr. Amit Cowshish	Additional Financial Adviser (A) & JS	23012915	131-A, South Block, New Delhi
Ms. Anuradha Mitra	Additional Financial Adviser (AM) &JS	23011871	130-B, South Block, New Delhi
Ms Shobhana Joshi	Additional Financial Adviser(S) & JS	23015429	134-A, South Block, New Delhi
Dr. S.C. Pandey	Additional Financial Adviser (P) & JS	23013557 23010159	537, DRDO Bhavan, New Delhi
Ms. Anuradha Prasad	Finance Manager (Maritime System) & JS	23014966	6, South Block, New Delhi
Mr. Vishvajit Sahay	Finance Manager (Land System) & JS	23012403	7, South Block, New Delhi
Smt. Dilip Biswas	Additional Financial Adviser (M) & JS	23012204	132, South Block, New Delhi
Ms. Vandana Srivastava	Finance Manager (Air)	23016759	205-C, South Block, New Delhi
Mr. Ramesh Kumar	Additional Financial Adviser(R) & JS	23015539	7-A, South Block, New Delhi.

DEPARTMENT OF DEFENCE PRODUCTION

NAME	DESIGNATION	TEL NO.(O)	OFFICE ADDRESS
Mr Raj Kumar Singh	Secretary (Defence Production)	23012527 23012300(FAX)	136, South Block, New Delhi
Mr Ajoy Acharya	Spl. Secretary (Defence Production)	23012470 23013133(FAX)	184-A South Block, New Delhi
Mr. T. Ramachandru	Joint Secretary (Supply)	23011553 23019961(FAX)	96-A South Block, New Delhi
Vacant	Joint Secretary (Coord)	23011593	23, A-Wing, Sena Bhavan,
Mr. Gyanesh Kumar	Joint Secretary (Shipyard)	23011219 23018538 (FAX)	134-B, South Block, New Delhi

Mr V. Soma Sundaran	Addl. Secretary (Ordnance Factories)	23013694 23017862(FAX)	184-B, South Block, New Delhi
Mr. Manoj Saunik	Joint Secretary (Aerospace)	23012778	133, South Block, New Delhi
Mr. Satyajeet Rajan	Joint Secretary (Export)	23015505	135-A, South Block, New Delhi
Mr. Ravinder Kumar Paul	Advisor (Cost)	23015734	23, Pt.III, South Block, New Delhi.

DEPARTMENT OF DEFENCE RESEARCH AND DEVELOPMENT ORGANISATION

NAME	DESIGNATION	DEPARTMENT	TEL NO.(O)	OFFICE ADDRESS
Mr. V.K. Saraswat	Scientific Advisor to RM & Secretary Defence Research and Development	Defence & Development	23011519	531, DRDO Bhawan, New Delhi

DEFENCE OFFSET FACILITATION AGENCY (DOFA)

NAME	DESIGNATION	TEL NO (O)	OFFICE ADDRESS
Mr Satyajeet Rajan	Chairperson (DOFA) & JS (X)	011-2301 5505 Email: jsx@nic.in	Room No. 135A, South Block, Ministry of Defence, New Delhi – 110011
Shri Saurabh Kumar	MemDirector(P&C) & Member Secretary, DOFA	011-2301 1420	Dte of Plg & Coord, DDP, Room.No.15, 'H' Block, New Delhi – 110011
Col K V Kuber	PO (CAP)	011-2379 2099	Dte of Plg & Coord, DDP, Ministry of Defence, Room No. 41, 'H' Block, New Delhi – 110011
Col Ravinder Singh	DPO (CAP)	011-2301 6272	Dte of Plg & Coord, DDP, Ministry of Defence, Room No. 12, 'H' Block, New Delhi – 110011

ANNEXURE – 9

DEFENCE PRODUCTION POLICY

1. Self-reliance in Defence is of vital importance for both strategic and economic reasons and has therefore been an important guiding principle for the Government since Independence. Accordingly, Government have, over the years assiduously built up capabilities in Defence R&D, Ordnance factories and Defence PSUs to provide our Armed forces with weapons/ ammunition/ equipment/ platforms and systems that they need for the defence of our country. Government considers that the industrial and technological growth in the past decades has made it possible to achieve this objective by harnessing the emerging dynamism of the Indian industry along with the capabilities available in the academia as well as research and development institutions.

2. Consequently, after careful consideration and in consultation with all stakeholders, Government have decided to put in place a Defence Production Policy. The objectives of the Policy are to achieve substantive self reliance in the design, development and production of equipment/ weapon systems/ platforms required for defence in as early a timeframe as possible; to create conditions conductive for the private industry to take an active role in this endeavour; to enhance

potential of SMEs in indigenization and to broaden the defence R&D base of the country. However, while pursuing the above objectives, the overall aim of ensuring that our forces have an edge over our potential adversaries at all times–in immediate terms as well as in sustainability–will be ensured. Accordingly, Government have decided that:-

3. Preference will be given to indigenous design, development and manufacture of defence equipment. Therefore, wherever the required arms, ammunition and equipment are possible to be made by the Indian industry within the timelines required by the Services, the procurement will be made from indigenous sources. Whenever the Indian industry is not in a position to make and deliver the equipment as per the SQRs in the requisite timeframe, procurement from foreign sources would be resorted to, in accordance with the Defence Procurement Procedure. While examining procurement cases, the time taken in the procurement and delivery from foreign sources vis-à-vis the time required for making it in the country, along with the urgency and criticality of the requirement will be examined as per the Defence Procurement Procedure before deciding to proceed with procurements from foreign sources.

4. Based on the approved Long Term Integrated Perspective Plan (LTIPP), equipment/weapon systems/ platforms required 10 years and further down the line will by and large be developed/integrated/made within the country. Sub-systems/equipment/ components that are not economically viable or practical to be made within the country may be imported, ensuring their availability at all times. However, as far as possible, the design and integration of the platform/system will be undertaken within the country.

5. Government will endeavour to build up a robust indigenous defence industrial base by, proactively encouraging larger involvement of the Indian private sector in design, development and manufacture of defence equipment. Towards this end, efforts would be made in progressively identifying and addressing any issue which impacts; or has the potential of impacting the competitiveness of the Indian defence industry in comparison to foreign companies.
6. In order to synergize and enhance the national competence in producing state of the art defence equipment/weapon systems/platforms within the price lines and timelines that are globally competitive; all viable approaches such as formation of consortia, joint ventures and public-private partnerships etc. within the Government approved frameworkwill be undertaken. The Academia, Research and Development Institutions as well as technical and scientific organizations of repute will be involved for achieving this objective.
7. Government will further simplify the procedures under the "MAKE" category of the Defence Procurement Procedure in such a manner that it enables the indigenous design and development of the required equipment/weapon systems/platforms by both public and private industry in a faster timeframe.
8. Service Headquarters (SHQs), while laying down the qualitative requirements for defence equipment/ weapon systems/platforms to be developed/ integrated/made, will exercise due diligence at all times to keep in view feasibility and practicability of the QRs. It will be ensured that the systems/platforms designed/developed/integrated in the country provide a competitive edge to our Services vis-à-vis our potential adversaries.

9. Government also recognizes that development of complex systems is generally a stage process with incremental changes progressing from Mk-I and Mk-II and so on. The stage process will be followed. However, at every review of such developmental projects by the Defence Production Board or Defence R&D Board as the case may be, it will be ensured that our equipment, weapons systems and platforms are such that they provide an edge to our forces over our potential adversaries. In case of delays in the realization of the projects, the corresponding proposal will be processed as per the Defence Procurement Procedure and the option of "Buy" shall be followed for the necessary numbers till indigenous production capability is established where after indigenous systems shall be procured.

10. Policies will be put in place to encourage the OFB, DPSUs and the Private Sector to strengthen their research and development wings so that constant up-gradation and improvement in systems under manufacture is possible.

11. Government will set up a separate fund to provide necessary resources to public/private sector including SMEs as well as academic and scientific institutions to support research and development of defence equipment/systems enhancing cutting edge technology.

12. In all cases of Transfer of Technology, DDP alongwith DRDO, HQIDS and SHQs will be involved in identification and evaluation of requisite technology, and subsequently would be responsible to ensure that appropriate absorption of technology takes place in the Indian industry. Thereafter, successive generations of the weapon systems/ platforms will be developed in the country.

13. Upgrades will be carried out by the Indian Industry as far as possible. DRDO, HQIDS, SHQs, OFB, DPSUs and the private sector will work in close coordination for continuous upgradation in systems.

14. The Committees set up under the Defence Procurement Procedure will process the acquisition proposals in accordance with the above policy guidelines.

15. The Raksha Mantri will hold an Annual Review of the progress in self-reliance that has been achieved during the year.

16. This Policy will come into force with immediate effect.

FREQUENTLY ASKED QUESTIONS (FAQS)

Q1. What is the procedure for the Indian firms to get Industrial Licence (IL) to be eligible to become offset partner?

Ans.
- The Government has allowed private sector participation upto 100 per cent in the defence industry sector with foreign direct investment (FDI) permissible upto 26 per cent.
- DPP 2008 has rationalised the industrial licensing procedure. The mandatory requirement of an industrial licence has been relaxed. The private sector will require licence only if so stipulated under the licensing requirement for defence industries issued by the department of industrial policy and promotion.
- The Secretariat of Industrial Assistance (Tel 011-23063088) can be contacted for any clarification regarding licence.
- Website of DIPP is **www.dipp.nic.in**

Q2. Does Indian government favour some industries versus others in choice of local industry partners?

Ans. Foreign vendor is free to choose the Indian Industrial partner.

Q3. Can an offset partner be changed midway?

Ans. Yes, they can be changed but only in exceptional cases with permission from the Ministry of Defence after giving valid reason.

Q4. What happens if the time schedule of meeting offset requirement is not adhered to?

Ans. A penalty of 5 per cent of the unfulfilled portion will be levied which the vendor will have to pay or else the same can be deducted from the bank guarantee of the main contract. It can also be deducted from the payable against the main contract.

Q5. What happens if vendor is finally not able to fulfill his obligation due to any reason?

Ans. Besides the penalty of 5 per cent on the unfulfilled portion, the vendor will also be liable to be disqualified for participation in future contract. This decision will however be taken after giving the vendor full opportunity to explain the reason for his failure.

Q6. What is the contact address of DOFA?

Ans. Contact address of DOFA is: -

DOFA Secretariat

Dte of Plg & Coord, DDP

Ministry of Defence

R. No. 15, 'H' Block

New Delhi - 110011

Email : **dofa-mod@nic.in**

Q7. Is DOFA constituted only from the Ministry or do they have other members also on board?

Ans. DOFA is a multi-disciplinary body which is represented by all stakeholders, viz, the services, DRDO, Industry associations, DPSUs/OFB and any other member as deemed necessary.

Q8. Is quantum of offsets prescribed at 30 per cent is indicative cost sacrosanct or can this figure be modified?

Ans. Initially only 30 per cent of indicative cost of proposal has been recommended. However, DAC reserves the right to increase this percentage in certain classes of cases depending upon the proposal under examination. Or it can even waive off the requirement for offset.

Q9. If a vendor takes initiative to provide a greater quantum of offset over and above the mandated 30 per cent will any preference or priority be given to such proposal?

Ans. All offset obligations of 30 per cent and above will be placed at par, and no extra benefit in any form will be given for obligations, which exceed the minimum prescribed limit.

Q10. Can the foreign vendor interact with DOFA prior to making offset proposals?

Ans. Yes, interactions by foreign vendors with DOFA is allowed and encouraged. They can be contacted at the following address/Telephone No.:-

(a) Postal - DOFA Secretariat
Dte of Plg & Coord, DDP
Ministry of Defence
R.No. 15, 'H' Block
New Delhi - 110011

(b) Telephone - 91-11-2301 5505, 91-11-23011420
91-11-2379 2099, 91-11-2301 6272

(c) Fax - 91-11-2301 5505, 91-1123709 3032

Q11. Is the foreign vendor free to contact anytime the Indian Industry or must they go only to the public sector (DPSU/OFB) ?

Ans. Foreign vendor is free to choose his Indian offset partner by making a choice from any of the DPSUs/ OFB or Indian private industry.

Q12. Which are the DPSUs/OFB? What are their contact details?

Ans. The details are as under :-

(a) OFB : The contact address of **Ordnance Factory Board** is as under
OFB : ofbtrade@vsnl.net
Ordnance Factory Board
10A, S.K. Bose Road
Kolkata 700 001
Tele : 033/22482730/22488439,
Fax : 033/22482927/22486647

(b) <u>BEL</u> : The contact address of **Bharat Electronics Limited** is as under :-

Bharat Electronics Limited
Outer Ring Road, Nagavara,
Bangalore – 560045
Ph. : 080-225039248, Fax : 080-225039286
E-mail : imd@bel-india.com,
Website : http://www.bel-india.com/

(c) <u>BEML</u> : The contact address of **Bharat Earth Movers Limited** is as under :-

Bharat Earth Movers Limited
Beml Soudha, 23/1, 4th Main
S.R Nagar, Bangalore – 560027
Ph : 080-22224457/3065/4141,
Fax : 080-22226883/4451

(d) <u>BDL</u> : The contact address of **Bharat Dynamics Limited** is as under :-

Bharat Dynamics Limited
Kanchanbagh, Hyderabad – 500 058
Ph : 040-24340712
Fax : 040-24340660
E-mail : bdbl@yahoo.com,
Website : //bdl/apnic.in
E-mail : beml@soudha.com,
Website : http://www.beml/ soudha.com

(e) <u>HAL</u> : The contact address of **Hindustan Aeronautics Limited** is as under :-

Hindustan Aeronautics Limited
15/1, Cubbon Road, Bangalore,
Ph : 080-22865197/5860
Fax : 080-22867140

E-mail : marketing@hal-india.com,

Website : http://www.hal-india.com/

(f) GSL : The contact address of **Goa Shipyards Limited** is asunder :-

Goa Shipyard Limited

Vasco Da Gama, Goa

Ph : 0832/2512152-56

Fax : 0832/2513260/2513943

E-mail : market@goashipyard.com,

Website : http://www.goashipyard.com/

(g) MIDHANI : The contact address of **Mishra Dhatu Nigam Limited** is as under :-

Mishra Dhatu Nigam Limited

Kanchanbagh, Hyderabad – 500 058

Ph : 040-24340634, Fax : 040-24340764

E-mail : hyd1 spralloy@sancharnet.in,

Website : www.ap.nic.in/midhani

(h) GRSE : The contact address of **Garden Reach Shipbuilers & Engineers Limited** is as under:-

43/46, Garden Reach Road

Kolkata – 700 024

Ph : 033-24698100 to 13,

Fax : 033-24698150/8144

E-mail : dsgrse@vsnl.net,

Website : http://www.grse.nic.in/

(i) MDL : The contact address of **Mazagon Dock Limited** is as under :-

Dockyard Road, Mazagon,

Mumbai – 400 010

Ph : 022-23738336,

Fax : 022-23738147

Abbreviations

(All the abbreviations given under have not necessarily been used in this book. These have been added because these are extensively used in Indian officialese)

AAP	Annual Acquisition Plan
Addl FA	Additional Financial Advisor
AFV	Armoured Fighting Vehicle
AGM	Annual General Meeting
AIP	Approval in Principle
AM	Acquisition Manager
AMC	Annual Maintenance Contract
AON	Acceptance of Necessity
AS	Additional Secretary
ASW	Anti-submarine Warfare
ATP	Acceptance Test Procedure
BC	Bank Commission
BEL	Bharat Electronics Ltd.
BEML	Bharat Earth Movers Ltd.
BFE	Buyer Furnished Equipment
BG	Bank Guarantee
CAE	Computer Aided Engineering
CAM	Computer Aided Machining
CAP	Capital Acquisition Plan
CCS	Cabinet Committee on Security
CD	Custom Duty
CDA	Controller of Defence Account
CFA	Competent Financial Authority
CFR	Cost and Freight

CIF	Cost Insurance and Freight
CII	Confederation of Indian Industry
CIP	Carriage and Insurance Paid to
CIR	Cargo Integration Review
CKD	Complete Knocked Down
CMD	Chairman & Managing Director
CNC	Contracts Negotiation Committee
COD	Central Ordnance Depot
COO	Commercial Offset Offer
COTS	Commercial Off the Shelf
CPT	Carriage Paid to
CST	Comparative Statement of Tenders
CTOT	Complete Transfer of Technology
CVD	Countervailing Duty
CWP&A	Controller of Warship Production and Acquisition
DAC	Defence Acquisition Council
DAO	Defence Acquisition Organization
DCF	Discounted Cash Flow
DD	Demand Draft
DDP	Department of Defence Production
DDP&S	Department of Defence Production & Supplies
DG	Director General
DGAQA	Director General of Aeronautical Quality Assurance
DGQA	Director General of Quality Assurance
DGS&D	Director General of Supply and Disposal
DIPP	Department of Industrial Policy & Promotion

DIR	Director
DOD	Department of Defence
DOFA	Defence Offset Facilitation Agency
DPB	Defence Procurement Board
DPP	Defence Procurement Procedure
DPSU	Defence Public Sector Unit
DRDO	Defence Research and Development Organisation
EFC	Expenditure Finance Committee
EIC	Equipment Induction Cell
EMC	Electro Magnetic Compatibility
EMI	Electro Magnetic Interference
EPC	Export Promotion Cell
ERV	Exchange Rate Variation
ESP	Engineering Support Package
EW	Electronic Warfare
FA	Financial Adviser
FAI	First Article Inspection
FDI	Foreign Direct Investment
FE	Foreign Exchange
FM	Financial Manager
FMECA	Failure Mode, Effect and Criticality Analysis
FOB	Free on Board
FPGA	Field Programmable Gate Array
GOI	Government of India
GSQR	General Staff Qualitative Requirement
HAL	Hindustan Aeronautics Ltd

HQ IDS	Headquarters Integrated Defence Staff
IAF	Indian Air Force
IDS	Integrated Defence Staff
IEC	Importer Exporter Code
IGA	Inter Governmental Agreement
IM	Indigenously Manufactured
INR	Indian Rupees
IP	Intellectual Property
IPL	Itemized Price List
ISO	International Organization for Standardization
ISPL	Illustrated Spare Part List
JRI	Joint Receipt Inspection
JS	Joint Secretary
JSQR	Joint Service Qualitative Requirement
JV	Joint Venture
L1	Lowest Bidder
LCA	Light Combat Aircraft
LOI	Letter of Intent
LRU	Line Replaceable Unit
LTPP	Long Term Perspective Plan
MET	Maintainability Evaluation Trial
MF	Main File
Mil	Military
MNCs	Multi National Companies
MoCA	Ministry of Civil Aviation
MoD	Ministry of Defence
MoU	Memorandum of Understanding

MRCA	Multi Role Combat Aircraft
MRLS	Manufacturer Recommended List of Spares
MRMR	Medium-Range Maritime Reconnaissance
MRO	Maintenance, Repair and Overhauling
MTBF	Mean Time Between Failure
MTBO	Minimum Time Before Overhaul
MTBUR	Mean Time Between Unit Replacement
MTTR	Mean Time to Repair
NCNC	No Cost No Commitment
NHQ	Naval Headquarters
NOC	No-objection Certificate
NPV	Net Present Value
O,I,D	Level Operator, Intermediate, Depot Level
OEM	Original Equipment Manufacturer
OF	Ordnance Factory
OFB	Ordnance Factory Board
OM	Office Memorandum
P&C	Planning & Coordination
PA	Production Agency
PBG	Performance Bank Guarantee
PCB	Printed Circuit Board
PDI	Pre Dispatch Inspection
PIB	Public Investment Board
POL	Petroleum, Oil and Lubricant
PROC	Procurement
PROM	Programmable Read Only Memory

PSO	Principal Staff Officer
PSR	Preliminary Staff Requirements
QA	Quality Assurance
QRSAM	Quick Reaction Surface to Air Missiles
R&D	Research and Development
RFI	Request for Information
RFP	Request for Proposal
RM	Raksha Mantri
SBAC	Society of British Aerospace Companies
SBI	State Bank of India
SCAP	Services Capital Acquisition Plan
SHQ	Service Headquarters
SKD	Semi Knocked Down
SMD	Storage Module Device
SMEs	Small and Medium Enterprises
SMT	Special Maintenance Tool
SOP	Standard Operating Procedure
SQR	Services Qualitative Requirement
SR	Short Refit
SRAM	Sideways Random Access Memory
SRU	Shop Replaceable Unit
SS	Special Secretary
STC	State Trading Corporation
STE	Special Test Equipment
TCA	Technical Collaboration Agreement
TEC	Technical Evaluation Committee
TEG	Technical Evaluation Group
TM	Technical Manager

TNC	Technical Negotiations Committee
TOEC	Technical Office for Engineering & Contracting
TOOC	Technical Offer Opening Committee
ToT	Transfer of Technology
TOTE	Table of Tools and Equipment
UAV	Unmanned Aeronautic Vehicle
USD	United States Dollars
UW	Under Water
WE	War Establishment
WLR	Weapon Locating Radar
WWR	War Wastage Reserve

DIRECTORY

AARTECH SOLONICS LTD

E2/57, Arera Colony, Bhopal, MP 462016 India

+91-755 2463593 91-755 2463593

vivek@aartechsolonics.com, info@aartechsolonics.com

Amit Raje, Managing Director; Vivek Ghanekar, National Marketing Manager Aartech is a System Solution Oriented R&D Enterprise in the field of Specialised and selected applied Energy Applications.

AARJAY INTERNATIONAL PVT LTD

948 B, 5th B Main Road, Vijaya Bank Layout, Bannerghatta Road, Bangalore-560076

43409200 43409299

aarjay@aarjay.com

P.K. Ramachandran, Managing Director

Aarjay International Pvt Ltd is a marketing associate of ELKAY INTERNATIONAL INC (USA). Focus areas are in the technology sectors of RF and Microwave, Optical, Electromechanical applied to the fields of telecom, aerospace, Defence, Automotive and Medical.

AEROTECHNICA CORP

2/19, Simirenka Str., Kyiv, 03134 Ukraine

00380444589263 00380444589424

www.aerotechnica.ua

info@aerotechnica.ua

Viktor Pogrebniak

Aerotechnica designs and manufactures advanced radar data acquisition and processing systems, automated command posts and control systems for air force, air Defence and Air traffic control.

Aerotechnica Offers:

1. Modernization of different models of radars.
2. Brand-new solid state radars for various applications.
3. Command posts for Air Force and Air Defence.
4. Modern automated ATC systems.

AERONICS EMAROH PVT LTD

782,7th Cross, Muthyala Nagar, Bangalore-560054

23459590, 23459590

www.aeronics.in

sathish@aeronics.in

Sathishkumar, Sales; Raghaughdra, Manufacturing

Aeronics Offers Contract Manufacturing Services in Assembly, Manufacture and repair of Electro-Mechanical/ Electronic. Aeronics Distributes High-Tech Components and Sub-Systems.

AIRBORNE SYSTEM

Llangeinor, Bridgend, CF32 8Pl, United Kingdom

+ 44 (0) 1656 727000

+ 44 (0) 1656 721100

www.airborne-sys.com

marking@airborne-sys.com

Richard Smallwood, Executive Vice President Customer Business; Ric Allion, Senior Vice President Customer Business (Europe)

Airborne Systems is the world leader in the design, development and manufacture of parachute systems for military personnel, aerial delivery systems and air droppable safety and survival equipment.

ALASKA STRUCTURES/ BLU-MED RESPONSE SYSTEMS

5808 Lk Washington Blvd,

Ste 215 Kirkland WA

(425)889-1205 (425)8891206

gb@alaskastructures.com

Don Diesel, Vice President,

Ken Mills-Representive

BLU MED response systems is the world's leader in Deployable medical facilities. BLU-MED's facilities include state-of- the-industry portable fabric shelters.

ALENIA AERONAUTICA

Via Campania 45, 00187 Rome, Italy

+ 39 - 06 - 420881

+ 39 - 06 - 42824528

asindici1@alenia.it

Mr. Stefano Tagliani, SVP - Media Comunicazione EImmagine

Alenia Aeronautica, a Finmeccanica group company, it designs and builds high performance combat aircraft, military and commercial transport aircraft, unmanned air systems, mission systems aircraft and modern aerostructures for airliners.

ALFAVARIA GROUP, S.R.O

Londýnská 78, Liberec, 46001,

Czech Republic

+(420) 485 100 303

+(420) 485 103 812

www.alfavaria.cz

info@alfavaria.cz

Jan Kupsky, CEO; Dagmar Chomova

Alfavaria Group introduces Mobile Service Workshops that it produces and delivers to military as well as civil sector.

AM GENERAL

105 N. Niles Ave, South Bend

IN 46617

AM general is the manufacturer of the high Mobility Multipurpose Wheeled Vehicle, or humvee® for U.S. and overseas military services.

AMDL/SYMMERTRICOM INC

65, Arun Complex, Dvg Road Basavangudi, Bangalore-4

080 - 42991800 080 - 26608785

tmi@amdlsed.com,shuba@amdlsed.com

K.S Sham Kumar, AGM

Symmetricom's products are used in major military projects of USA such as tactical communication Network, Military Vehicles, and radars etc.

ANALOGIC CONTROLS INDIA LTD

6-1-190/25, Padmarao Nagar, Secunderabad 500 025

91 - 40 - 27505768 91 - 40 - 27504776

acil@analogiccontrols.com

K Padmanabhan, Managing Director; Pradeep Dhar

ACIL is a leader in Rugged Systems, Embedded Systems, Data acquisition, Data Logging, Special Test & Measurement Equipments.

ANTONOV AERONAUTICAL SCIENTIFIC & TECHNICAL COMPLEX

1, Tupolev Str., Kyiv, 03062, Ukraine

+ 38 044 454-31-49;

+ 38 044 454-32-33

+ 38 044 400-81-44

www.antonov.com

info@antonov.com

Dmytro Kiva, Chief Executive Officer (General Designer)

ANTONOV works on the program of the IAF AN-32 transports upgrading. The new transport version of AN-74 can carry various cargoes including military-purpose ones with a total weight up to 10 t.

ASSOCIATED COMPOSITE MATERIALS (PVT) LTD

17, Community Centre, New Friends Colony, New Delhi 110065, India

0091 - 11 - 41672741

0019 - 11 - 41672742.

http://www.acmprotection.com

info@acmprotection.com

Mr. Arjun Nath, Managing Director; Mr. Bhushan Arora, President-Operations

M/s. Associated Composite is having diversified interest in manufacturing composites, Engineering solutions, technical textiles for industrial applications.

ASTRA MICROWAVE PRODUCTS LTD

Astra Towers, Survey No. 12(P), Kothaguda Post, Opp. CII Green Building, Hitech City, Kondapur, Hyderabad - 500084

+ 91 40 30618000 +91 40 30618048

sales@astramwp.com

B. Malla Reddy, Managing Director

Astra Microwave Products Limited (AMPl) is one of the leading designers and manufacturers of high quality R.F. & Microwave Modules and sub-systems in India.

ASTRUM

Stanhope, Co. Durham, DL13 2YR

01388 528248 01388 528879

info@astrum.uk.com

Mr Ray Jeffries, Mr Gary Neasham, Mr Anwar Shaikh

Astrum has been manufacturing track solutions and high integrity structural castings for AFVS for over 70 years and is widely recognised as a world leading authority on track and running gear design and manufacture.

ATLAS ELEKTRONIK GMBH

Sebaldsbruecker Heerstr. 235 28309 Bremen

+ 49 421 457-02 + 49 421 457-3699

http://www.atlas-elektronik.com

marketing@atlas-elektronik.com

Atlas has a broad offering of sonars and sensors, command and control systems for submarines and surface combatants, mine countermeasures systems, unmanned underwater vehicles, radio and communications equipment, naval weapons as well as coastal protection and traffic guidance systems.

AVEC CHEM S.R.O.

Stare Jesencany 79, 530 02 Pardubice, Czech Republic

+ 420 466 303 037

+ 420 466 303 037

info@avec.cz

Mr. Michal Filipi, Executive Head

AVEC CHEM specializes in the development and production of CBRN personal protective equipment (PPE) and air and water-treatment equipment.

AVIO SPA

Via 1 Maggio, 99, 10040 Rivalta Di Torino, Italy

+ 39 011 0084319 + 39 011 0084163

cristiana.aimonerondo@aiogroup.com

Ms. Cristiana Aimone Rondo, Public Relations & Communication

AVIO designs, develops and produces modules and components for propulsion systems for aircraft and helicopters. Avio is Italian champion in aeroengines and world leader in mechanical transmissions.

AZIMUTH TECHNOLOGIES LTD

15 Hataasiah. Raanana 43654

972-9-7612500 972-9-7408767

mkt@azimuth.co.il

Shlomo Reisman, Yosef Gonen, Ziv Ashkenaki

Azimuth Technologies Ltd. is a world leader in target acquisition, fire coordination, navigation, and orientation solutions for defense applications.

AGUSTA WESTLAND PRODUCT & DETAILS

OSS Air Management Pvt Ltd (Service Providers for Agusta Helicopters in India), Juhu, Mumbai, India

Tel: +91 22 2202 6413

Paolo Girasole, Head Finmeccanica

Agusta Westland is a helicopter design and manufacturing company. Its product range includes: Light Helicopter, Intermediate Helicopter, Medium Helicopter and Medium - Heavy Helicopter.

ALENIA AERONAUTICA PRODUCT & DETAILS

N-57, Panchsheel Park, New Delhi-110017, India

Paolo Girasole Head Finmeccanica India

Alenia Aeronautica is an aerospace engineering company that designs, builds and certifies military and commercial aircraft and mission systems, including unmanned air vehicles. Some of the world's most sophisticated aircraft, including the Eurofighter Typhoon,

C-27J, ATR42MP and ATR72 ASW, are built in Alenia plants.

ADIGEAR INTERNATIONAL AND PROTECTIVE PRODUCTS INTERNATIONAL, USA. (JOINT VENTURE PARTNER)

A-40, Mayapuri Indl. Area, Ph-I,

New Delhi - 110064

011-40797000 011- 41833637

www.adigear.com

adigear@vsnl.com

Mr. Sandeep Khanna, Director Adigear International

Its body armor and vehicle armor division manufactures and supplies bullet proof jackets, vests, helmets, blankets etc.The other security equipments include high altitude suits, combat suits, fire retardant overall and coverall. The company has also entered into a joint venture partnership with M/s Protective Product International, USA being the third largest supplier to the U.S.

ADVENTURES (INDIA) PVT LTD

M-56, Greater Kailash-II,

New Delhi. + 011-29221357

www.adventuresltd.in

marketing@adventuresltd.in

Syed Kashif

Adventures (India) Pvt. Ltd represents some of the world's leading manufacturers of internationally known brands of ropeways, mountaineering equipment, all purpose clothing, tents rucksacks, sleeping bags, flood mountain & avalanche rescue equipments etc.

AERIAL SERVICES

Hanger No 1, Juhu Airport,

Mumbai 400054

91-22-26156909 / 2661 3626

www.asplindia.in

asplgps@vsnl.net , sales@asplindia.in

Mr. A.M Lalljee, Director 9820106100/91-22-26156707/ 26156696

The authorized Distributors in India for Garmin International Inc. USA manufacturers of global Positioning systems and OEM sensor boards.

AGMATEL INDIA PVT LTD

E-366, Second Floor, Nirman Vihar, Vikas Marg, Delhi-110092

+91 9810054741-42 +91 11 22019833

marketing@agmatel.com

Mr. Anand Kumar Aggarwal, Director; Mr. Vijay Kumar Malhotra, Director

Agmatel India Private limited is a leading organization in the field of sales and Marketing of high precision test & Measurement instruments and advanced information technology products.

ALKAN SAS

Rue Du 8 Mai 1945 - 94450

Valenton, France

+33 1 45 10 86 89 +33 1 45 10 86 39

www.alkan.fr

info@alkan.fr

ALKAN SAS is a French military aeronautical equipment manufacturer. ALKAN have the mastery of weapon carriage and ejection equipment.

AMPHENOL INTERCONNECT INDIA PVT LTD

105 Bhosari Industrial Area,

Pune - 411025 & 1414,

Chiranjeev Tower, Nehru Place,

New Delhi

011-26449177 020-30688321

www.amphenol-in.com

sales@amphenol-in.com

Sunil Kumar Yadav

Amphenol India deals in interconnect systems for Military, aerospace and harsh environment application, design and manufacture high performance cylindrical connectors, rectangular connectors, Pcb connectors, EMi/EMP filter connectors, high voltage connectors, fiber Optics connectors, back shells, cable assemblies, integrated sub systems and large varieties of special application connectors.

ANDHRA ELECTRONICS LTD

34 & 35, IDA,

Kakinada - 533005, India.

+91-884-2342203/2341850/2379407

+91-884-2341145/2379408

info@andhraelec.com

Mr. K.V. Sri Ram, Executive Director

Andhra Electronics is the manufacturer of Professional grade frequency control Products, Rf & Microwave Components/Modules for telecommunication, Military and space applications.

ANJANI TECHNOPLAST LTD

6A, Sector 40/41 Ecotec-1,
Greater Noida - 201301
0120 4789056 120 4789059
www.anjani.com
lokesh@anjani.com,hemant@anjani.com
Mr Lokesh Gupta,
Manager - Marketing 9811169267

Company engaged in the areas of light Weight bullet-Proof Jackets, bullet Proof helmets, bullet Proof Panels for Vehicles, bullet Proof shield, riot Protection Equipment, light Weight stretcher for Defence & Paramilitary forces.

ARSENAL 2000 JSCO

100, Rozova Dolina Str,
6100 Kazanlak, Bulgaria
+35943150000 +35943150001
arsenal2000@arsenal2000-bg.com
Mr. Rajeev Agarwal, Managing Director

ARSENAL 2000 JSCO. is the general trade representative of arsenal Jsco., bulgaria. line of business of Arsenal JSCO. ; Design, Production,engineering and trade of armaments, small arms artillery ammunition, purotechnic products, hunting and sport Weapon and ammition, Machine tools and tooling.

ASHOK LEYLAND

www.ashokleyland.com
vinod.chacko@ashokleyland.com
Vinod Chacko, DGM - Corp
Communication 98414 16233

The company's product range spans from 7.5 T GVW to 49T GTW in goods transport and from 19 seaters to 80 seaters in passenger transport, apart from a host of special application vehicles and diesel engines.

BAEHAL SOFTWARE LTD

Airport Lane, Hal Estate,
Bangalore -560017
080-25228683/6332 080-25220915
marketing@baehal.com
Manjunath H V, Head Business Development +91 9880194069; Venkatesh H, Business Development +91 9845041227

Baehal Software is a joint venture between Hindustan Aeronautics Ltd and BAE systems provides it solutions and services (both hardware and software) to aerospace and Defence .

BARCO

A-38, B&C, Sector-64,
Noida, UP-India
+ 91 120 4020000 + 91 120 4020100
sales.besl@barco.com
Vivekanand, Sales Director; Lokesh Malhotra, Business Development Manager (Defence)

Barco, a global technology company, designs and develops visualization solutions for a variety of selected professional markets: medical imaging, media and entertainment, infrastructure and utilities, traffic and transportation, defence and security, education and training, simulation and virtual reality.

BAUER KOMPRESSOREN INDIA PVT LTD

A-71/72,"H" Block, Midc Pimpri,
Pune 411 018, Maharashtra, India
+ 91-020-65108777

+ 91-020-27487000

www.bauergroup.com

info@bauer-kompressoren.in

BAUER KOMPRESSOREN, is in the business of high pressure compressor systems.

BCB INTERNATIONAL LTD

Unit 7 & 8 Clydesmuir Rd Ind Est, Cardiff, CF24 2QS, United Kingdom

+44 29 2043 3700 +44 29 2043 3701

bs@bcbin.com

Peter Holmes, Sanjay Bhardwaj

BCB international are manufacturer and designer of Personal combat Equipment.

BERETTA - FABBRICA D'ARMI PIETRO BERETTA

Via P. Beretta 18, Gardone VT,

Brescia, Italy

+39-030-8341404 +39-030-8341355

paolo.sebastiani@beretta.com

Gianluca Baldassarre, Defence & Law Enforcement Sales Director

The group manufactures advanced firearms, optics and accessories

BETH-EL ZIKHRON YAAQOV INDUSTRIES LTD

P.O. Box 166, 1 Avshalom Road 30900 Zikhron Yaaqov, Israel

+972 4 6299947 +972 4 6299900

j.fehlauer@beind.com

Jehudah Fehlauer

Beth-El Zikhron Yaakov Industries Ltd. is a world leader for designing and manufacturing collective Nbc-Protection systems

BOEING

P.O. Box 516.., St. Louis, Missouri, USA

+1-314-232-0232 +972 4 6299900

www.boeing.com

Vivek Lall, Vice President; Brian Nelson, Communications , 10th Floor, Eros Corporate Tower, Nehru Place, New Delhi-110019,

91-11-46566950, F: 91-11-46566002

Boeing is the world's leader in space and defense business and the world's largest and most versatile manufacturer of military aircraft. Boeing is also the world's largest satellite manufacturer, an emerging leader in support systems and services, and a leading global supplier of human space exploration systems and services.

BRUKER DALTONICS LTD

Banner Lane, Coventry, Cv4 9gh

011-26786141 011-26786142

ravi.mawkin@bdal.in

Ravi Mawkin

Bruker Detection a global leader in CBRN detection, manufactures a wide range of chemical, biological and Nuclear Radiation Detectors.

BAE SYSTEMS PIC

2nd Floor, Hotel Le Meridien Commercial Tower, Raisina Road,

New Delhi 110001

91-11-43412345, 43412400,

F:911-43412373/74

marksimpkins@baesindia.com, mark.simpkins@baesystems.com

Mr Mark Simpkins, VP & General Manager, BAE Systems - India

BAE Systems is a defence and aerospace company that has global interests particularly in North America through its subsidiary BAE

Systems Inc. The major systems are Air Frames, Land Systems, and Naval Projects

BOMBARDIER

B 301-307, Somdutt Chamber, 15 Bhikaji Cama Place, R.K. Puram West, New Delhi-110066

Suman Bose, Country Director - India Bombardier Transport India Limited

Bombardier is a Global Transportation Company. It designs, manufactures, sells and supports the widest range of world class products in the Aircraft and Rail equipment sectors such as Commercial and Business Jets as well as Rail Transportation Equipment, Systems and Services.

BABCOCK INTERNATIONAL GROUP

15/B, Kamal Kunj, Lrla Bridge, S.V Road, Andheri-West, Mumbai-400058

Part of Babcock International Group, Marine Division - integrated technology provides platform design, integration and management services and high integrity systems to the marine, oil and gas and defence sectors.

BAE SYSTEMS

6 Carlton Gardens, London, Sw1y 5ad, London

44 1252 384736 44 1252 383107

richard.J.humphreys@baesystems.com

richard humphreys

BAE Systems is the premier global defence, security and aerospace company delivering a full range of products and services for air, land and naval forces, as well as advanced electronics, security, information technology solutions and customer support services.

BHARAT ELECTRONICS LTD

Outer Ring Road, Nagavara, Bangalore-560008

91(080)25039300 91(080)25039291

corpcomn@bel.co.in

Mr E A Hariharan

Communication systems, surveillance and security related equipment. Product range includes man portable and operable rapidly deployable unmanned aerial vehicle system, advanced high performance fast attack crafts, Night Vision Devices, interception and monitoring equipments for on-going radio communication via GSM/CDMA/ Satellites/ HF/VHF/UHF communication system.

BHE BONN HUNGARY ELECTRONICS LTD

Foti Str. 56. Budapest,

H-1047 Hungary

+36 1 233 2138 +36 1 233-2506

www.bhe-mw.eu

info@bhe-mw.eu

BHE Develops and Manufactures RF and Microwave products for government, defence and space applications.

BRAHMOS AEROSPACE

praveenpathak@brahmos.com

Praveen Pathak,

Addl GM (Mkt Promotion)

919810644473

BrahMos aerospace is a Joint Venture between India and Russia to design, develop, produce and market supersonic cruise missile weapon complexes.

BROADCAST ENGINEERING CONSULTANTS INDIA LTD

Plot No. 7, Factory Road, Near Safdarjung Hospital, New Delhi 110029

011-4315 4315 011-4315 4316

becil@vsnl.com

Deepak Ranjan Gogoi,

Joint General Manager

+91 11 23378824

BECIL is a govt. of India Enterprise is a turnkey solution Provider in the field of satellite communication systems, surveillance and security related equipment.

BUMAR SP. Z O

Al. Jana Pawla II No. 11 00-828 Warsaw, Poland

48 22 31125 12 48 22 311 26 42

bumar@bumar.com

The offer of Bumar covers mainly:

- radar systems for air space surveillance
- anti - aircraft missiles and artillery systems
- heavy armored vehicles and infantry transporters
- optoelectronic equipment

BURCKHARDT COMPRESSION (INDIA) PVT LTD

Gat No. 304, Village Kondhapuri, Pune-Nagar Road, Tal. Shirur,

Dist. Pune.

02137-669400 02137-669496

avinash.chougule@burckhardt

compression.com

Mr. Vinod Kumar Sharma, Regional Manager - North; Mr. Abhay Gulvani, Vice President- Sales & Marketing

Burckhardt Compression India is a wholly owned subsidiary of Burckhardt compression AG, Switzerland, one of the world's largest manufacturers of reciprocating compressors.

CALVI SPA

Via IV Novembre 2, 23807

Merate, Lecco, Italy

+39 039 99851 +39 039 9985240

vito.liva@calvi.it

Vito Liva, Sales Manager

Special steel profiles cold drawn according to customer's drawing. Calvi's profile can be used in main applications, like fire arms, linear guides, automotive components, textile, machine tools, agricultural machines, etc.

CARL ZEISS OPTRONICS

Carl Zeiss Strasse 22

+49 7364 20 65 30 +49 7364 20 36 97

optronics@zeiss.com

Mr. Andreas Plaznik, Mr. Carsten Batz, Mr. Harald Hansen, Mr. Brad Dann

Carl Zeiss Optronics designs, develops and produces state-of-the-art optronic instruments for military and civilian applications.

CENTRE FOR DEVELOPMENT OF TELEMATICS

C-Dot Campus, Mehrauli.

New Delhi- 110030

011-26802856 011-26803338

cdot@cdot.co.in

Sh. B.S Chauhan, GM - Systems 9810998055; Ms. Sonia Tolani, Manager-BPM 9818400616

Centre for Development of Telematics (C-DOT), a premier telecom technology development centre of government of India, has been a pioneer and a nation builder. C-DOT has developed products and technologies in TDM, ATM switches, NGN, IN, SDH, DWDM, GPON, satellite communi-cations, and broadband access.

CESKA ZBROJOVKA A.S.

Svat. Cecha 1283, 688 27 Uhersky Brod, Czech Republic

+420 572 655 113 +420 572 633 811

skrabal@czub.cz

Jiri Skrabal, Sales Manager 420-737226053; Surrender Data, Technical Advisor 00-91- 91 11 23746506

The current line of Ceska Zbrojovka products includes sporting and hunting firearms as well as duty weapons for armed forces, police and other armed units.

CHEM-VERSE CONSULTANTS (INDIA) PVT LTD

120/5, Jasood Bhavan, Road No.24A, Sion (West), Mumbai-400022

24095503/24033387 24097858

sales@chemverse.com

Mr. N.C. Mavani, Managing Director; Mr. D.G. Kamath, Head-Sales & Marketing

Chem-Verse Consultants (India) Pvt. Ltd. has full fledged oil blending, grease compounding and aerosol filing lines with fully equipped R&D and Quality control laboratory.

CHERMING GROUP PLC

Cherming House 1500 Parkway, Solent Business Park Way Whiteley Po157AF

01489881880 01489881123

info@cherming.co.uk

Chemring is a global group of companies that specializes in the manufacture of energetic material products and decoy countermeasures.

CLEARTRAIL TECHNOLOGIES PVT LTD

89, Nehru Place, 9th Floor, 901/A Hemkunt Chambers,

New Delhi 110019

0120 4092100 0120 409 2140

anurag.khasgiwala@clear-trail.com

Manohar Katoch, Sr. Director - Business Development

Clear Trail is an Indian company providing lawful interception and analysis solutions to lEA's, intelligence agencies and communication service Providers.

COLT DEFENSE LLC

PO Box 118 Hartford, Ct 06141 USA

1-800-962-2658 1-860-244-1381

jradziwon@colt.com

Michaels P. Reissig, Vice President; Col. Gautam Sethi, Country Manager.

Colt rifles and carbines 5.56mm (223 REM) have been truly battle-tested under every condition.

CONTROP ISRAEL

P.O Box 611, Hod Hashron 45105, Israel

972-9-744-0661 972-9-744-0662

marcom@controp.co.il

Meir Giber, Director, Sales & Marketing; Shlomo Nir, General Manager

Controp specializes in the development and production of Electro- Optical and Precision Motion control systems.

CRYOGENIC & VACUUMSYSTE-MSINCL. SIBAT

En Harod Thud, Israel 18960

4530843 46532424

marketing@ricor.com

Yoar Zur

RICOR is a world leader in the field of development and manufacturing miniature stirling cryogenic coolers.

CUBIC SIMULATION SYSTEMS INCORPORATED

2001 W, Oak Ridge, Road, Orlando Fl 32809-3809, USA

+1 407 859 7410 +1 407 855 4840

cubicinfo@cubic.com

Thomas Alexander Scott, Director; Mark Andrew Saturno, Director - Business Development

Cubic is the world leader in the field of live, Virtual and constructive training.

CYBERMOTION TECHNOLO-GIES PVT LTD

Plot No:235, Road No: 14,

Banjara Hills, Hyderabad-500034

040-23557091/92/93 040-23557094

anand@cybermotionind.com

Anand Jambholkar; Praveen Jambholkar

Cybermotion technologies have number of automation products like DSP based Digital controllers, BLDC motor, electro mechanical actuator Planetary gear box, ball and roller screw Mechanism.

CADES

100/1, Anchorage, Richomond Road, Bangalore -560025, India

+91-80-41939000 +91-80-41939099

info@cadestech.com

Cades is one of leading product Design and Engineering Services Companies catering to Aerospace, Defence and Automotive sectors.

CAE

8585 cote De liesse

danmar@cae.com

Chris Shellwag, Director -

Communication

108, 3rd, Floor, Gavipuram Guttahalli, Off. Bull Temple Road,

Bangalore-560019, P: 91 80 2625 600, Email: drramesh@macment.com

CAE is a leading provider of simulation and modeling technologies and integrated training solutions for defence customers worldwide.

CARINEX LTD

51. Nagyszõlõs STR, h-1113 Budapest, Hungary

+36 1 386 8667, +36 1 386 8569 +36 1 386 8666

www.carinex.hu

info@carinex.hu

HF, VHF/UHF, SHF radio reconnaissance and Direction finding equipment/ systems; terrestrial microwave and satellite monitoring systems; Nationwide communications monitoring systems (lawful interception); audio and video surveillance equipment/systems; vehicle-, object- and person tracking systems.

CENTUM GROUP

44, Khb Industrial Area, Yelahanka New Town, Bangalore – 560106, Karnataka, India

+91 9448281868 , +91 80 4143 6071 +91 80 4143 6005

www.centumelectronics.com

csmenon@centumelectronics.com

Sreekumar Menon, General Manager-Sales and Marketing

Centum provides customers with customized product design, development, manufacturing, service and component solutions for high reliability applications.

CENZIN CO. LTD

81/83 Czerniakowska Street, 00-957 Warsaw - Poland

+48 22 43 44 133 +48 22 43 44 163

www.cenzin.eu

cenzin@cenzin.com.pl

Foreign Trade Enterprise CENZIN Co. Ltd. - the state owned company – is the oldest Polish company dealing with the export and import of armament, military equipment and technology.

CLOUD CAP TECHNOLOGY, INC

2621 Wasco Street Hood River, OR 97031 USA

+1 541 387 2120 +1 541 387 2030

kelly.garcia @goodrich.com

Pierce Louis, Business Development

PhD, Site Director

Cloud Cap Technology, Inc. is a leading provider of proprietary end-to -end avionics solutions for small unmanned aerial vehicles (uaV) and sensors for manned vehicles. Primary products include autopilot flight management systems, inertial measurement sensors and stabilized imaging micro-gimbals.

COBHAM PLC

Brook Road, Wimborne, Dorset, BH21 2BJ UK

+44 1202 882020 +44 1202 849401

info@cobham.com

Room 265, Hyatt Regency, Bhikaji Cama Place, Ring Road, New Delhi-110607, P: +91-11-66771498/1499, Email:vagishchandra.gaur@cobham.com

Cobham is provider of advanced digital military vehicle intercom systems, an integral part of the c4isr and battlefield digitization programmes.

COMROD

Regus House, George Curl Way, Southampton SQ182RZ

0047 95875555 +1 541 387 2030

sales@comrod.com

Niklas Hermansson, President and CEO, 0047 95875555

Comrod is a Norwegian company experience in the design and manufacture of antennas for the defence market covering the HF, VHF and UHF frequency bands.

CONCORD SAFETY SOLUTIONS PVT LTD

Khasra No. 3963, Lal Tappar Indl. Area, Dehradun-Haridwar Highway, Dehradun (Uttaranchal)-248140. India

+91 135 2499169 +91 9634270107

Contact @Concordsafety.Com

Anurag Tripathi, Manager-Corporate Communications

Concord Safety Solutions Pvt. Ltd. is a joint venture manufacture state of art armored vehicles in India.

CBS-CENTRIFUGES, BIO TOILETS, AND OIL CLEANING MACHINES

48-C PKT-C, SFS Flats, Mayur Vihar Phase-3, Delhi-110096. India

+91-11-22613408 +91-11-22613362

cbsenergy@gmail.com

Cbs Technologies Pvt Ltd Manufactures:

1. CENTRIFUGAL OIL FILTER
2. PORTABLE OIL CLEANING CENTRIFUGE MACHINES
3. BIO-TOILETS
4. ENAMELED WIRES (COPPER AND ALMUNIUM)

DAKO-CZ, A.S.

Budovatelu 323, 538 43 Tremosnice, Czech Republic

+420 469 617 111 +420 469 617 116

dako-cz@dako-cz.cz

Mr. Milan Polak, Chairman of the Board of Directors & MD

DAKO-CZ, A.S. is a trading and manufacturing company with focus on air pressure brake systems for all types of railway vehicles, and hydraulic and other systems and parts for military use, as stabilizing system, bogie control device for T-72 tank, lubricating and control system for BVP-I armoured vehice, etc.

DATA PATTERNS (INDIA) PVT LTD

105, 10th Cross Indiranagar 1st Stage, Bangalore - 560 038

+91 80 4242 4141 +91 80 4242 4142

www.datapatterns.co.in

mkt@datapatterns.co.in

R. Soundararajan, Sr. Vice President; S. Rangarajan, Managing Director

Data Patterns has a wide range of technology competence in domains such as radars, avionics, fire control, Weapon Electronics, control and Navigation.

DCNS

Laurent Videau Delegate- India & Thailand,

H/P : 91 9810231094, P: 91 11 43531920 fAX: 91 11 43531949, email: laurent@videau.com

DCNS is a leading European player on the world market for naval defence systems. The group designs, builds and supports surface ships, submarines and mission-critical systems and equipment incorporating the most advanced technologies.

D & M INDIA [WEIBEL RADARS]

201a, Supermart 2, DLF Phase -4, Gurgaon - 122002, Haryana

+91 124 4085652 +91 124 4086640

sales@dmintrade.com

Praveen Mehra, Director; Krishna Kumar, Technical Manager

Five types of Radar available with Weibel Tactical Muzzle Velocity Radars Systems Fixed Head Doppler Radar Systems Azimuth & Elevation Monopulse Tracking Radar Systems. Multi-Frequency Long Range Tracking Radar Systems.

DRS TECHNOLOGIES

1110 West Hibiscus Boulevard 32901 Melbourne, USA

+321-727-3672 +321 725 0496

crobinson@drs-ts.com

Carrie Robinson, Marketing Manager

DRS Technologies is a world leader in high-performance ultra-rugged computer systems designed to operate in harsh military environments.

DSM DYNEEMA

Mauritslaan, 49-6129 El Urmond, P.O Box 1163 6160 Bd Geleen, The Netherlands

91-124-4799004/267 91-124-4179850

www.dyneema.com,

www.dyneemamatters.com

sandeep.saigal@dsm.com

Sandeep Saigal, Marketing Manager-Vehicle Protection, Life Protection Asia Pacific +91 9999913765

DSM Dyneema is the inventor and manufacturer of Dyneema®, the world's strongest fiber TM. Dyneema® is an ultra strong polyethylene fiber that offers maximum strength combined with minimum weight. Key applications for Dyneema® are highly diverse and range from bullet resistant vests, inserts and helmets to anti-ballistic protection vehicles for both military and police use.

DURATUF GLASS INDUSTRIES PVT LTD

38/4 Jakhoda Village, Rohtak Road,

Bahadurgarh-124507, Haryana

1276-241179/80/81 1279-241566

gulatiglass@gmail.com

Sandeep Saigal, Marketing Manager

Duratuf Glass Industries Pvt.Ltd. is India's leading Glat and curved glass producer. They supply full range of glasses for automobiles, security and bullet resistance glass for automobile and buildings both in India and abroad under brand name of Duratuf & DURASAFE.

DYNALOG (INDIA) LTD

U-1, Ground Floor, Green Park (Main), New Delhi-110016

011-26524841 011-26524838

hdubey@dynalogindia.com

Akshey S Adhalrao, Managing Director

Design, development and fabrication of defense electronics include development of various types of Mil grade CPU boards, memory boards, communication boards etc.

DASSAULT SYSTEMS

138, Jor Bagh, Dassault House,

New Delhi - 110003

P: 91-11-24652464

E: raopv@vsnl.com

Mr Alain Remaudiere, Area Marketing & Sale Gm Dassault Aviation

Dassault Systems develops and markets Product Lifecycle Management application software and services that support industrial processes and provide a 3D vision of the entire lifecycle of products from conception to maintenance.

DASSAULT AVIATION

138, Jor Bagh, Dassault House,

New Delhi - 110003

P: 91-11-24652464, + 91 112 465 24 65, Fax· + 91 112 465 24 64, www.dassault-aviation.com

Dassault Aviation is a French aircraft manufacturer of military, regional and business jets, a subsidiary of Dassault Group. Its prodcts include: Rafale, Jaguar, Atlantique, UAVs, Falcon family (5versions).

DENEL LTD

Suite 1131 Maurya Shereton Hotel & Towers, Diplomatic Enclave New Delhi- 110021

Tel: 91-011-23023029/30 Fax 91-011-23023241 Email: alinai@vsnlcom

Denel Ltd operates in the Military Aerospace and Landward Defence Environment. It supplies Aircraft MRO, Aircraft Production and Component Manufacturing, Artillery Projectiles, Light Weapons, Artillery Propulsion, Artillery Systems, Heavy Calibre Ammunition Mine Action and Contraband, etc.

DASS HITACHI LTD

8/9th Mile Stone G.T Road,

P.O. Mohan Nagar, Ghaziabad

0120-4755200, 0120-4755200,

011-23010128

dhl@dasshitachi.com

The company is recognized by the Ministry of Science and Technology as an independent research and development unit. The company specializes in executing turnkey projects on single window concept in the field of Nuclear, Biological and Chemical Warfare.

DEUTSCH

104, Ground Floor, Prestige Omega, 1st Phase, Epip Zone, Whitefield, Bangalore-560 066, India

+91 80 404 66 500/501/513/520/522

+91 80 404 66 505

mthomas@deutsch.net

Mrs. Mariamma Thomas, Asst. Manager-Sales Execution

Product range includes connectors and contacts, cables and assemblies, accessories etc.

DIEHL DEFENCE CORPORATE DIVISION

Alte Nubdorfer Str 13, Uberlingen

49 7551 896945 49 7551 8976945

stefan.wegis@diehl-defence.de

Stefan Wegis

The product spectrum ranges from guided missiles for army, air force and navy, intelligent munition solutions up to reconnaissance, self-protection and training systems.

DRDO

Rajaji Marg, New Delhi-11

91-11-23013209,23015291 91-11-23793008

radkrishnan@hqr.drdo.in

Mr S Radhakrishnan, Director - DIITM

DRDO's mission is technical self reliance in defence systems and weapons. It has the mandate to design, develop and lead to production, state-of-the-art weapon systems, platforms, customised solutions, sensors and allied equipment to meet the requirements of the Indian armed forces and provide support in the area of human potential to improve combat effectiveness of the troops.

EAST WEST ENGINEERING COMPANY

58, Sharda Niketan, Pitampura,

New Delhi - 110034

9811054460 27018936

www.safefireindia.co.in

defence@safefireindia.co.in

Vaibhav Gupta, Director

Company obtained worldwide right in 2003 for manufactures non-electric automatic fire detection and suppression systems suitable for fire protection of vehicles, aircraft and micro-environments.

EGO ZLIN, SPOL. S R.O.

U Pekarny 438,763 14 Zlin - Stipa Czech Republic

(+420) 577 100 031

(+420) 577 914 363

www.egozlin.cz

obchod@egozlin.cz

The company is a leading Czech supplier of special mobile workplaces and systems for biological detection and protection including complete logistic support.

ELECTRONICS CORPORATION OF INDIA LTD

Ecil P.O., Hyderabad - 500062,

Andhra Pradesh

040-27120671 040-27120671

bhagavantam@ecil.co.in

Shri Y.S. Mayya, Chairman & Managing Director.

ECIL has evolved into a multi-product, multi technology and multi-disciplinary company with products and services in strategic sectors of Nuclear, Defence, space, security, civil aviation, information and broadcasting, telecommunications, Oil and gas, Power, e-governance, Education and Export sectors.

ELEKTRONIK LAB

10 A Masilamani Street, T Nagar, Chennai - 600017

044-24310156 044-24322819

info@elektroniklab.com

Mr. Nanda Kumar, CEO

Elektronik lab integrates complex communications and navigation systems, and ensures that these are optimally maintained through a nationwide after sales support network including all major ports of India.

ELETTRONICA

Via Tiburtina Valeria Km 13.7 - 00131

+39.0641541 +39.064154924

www.elt-roma.com

Candidoro Giannicchi, V P - Business Development

ELETTRONICA, specialises in Electronic Warfare systems: RWR, ESM, ECM and ELINT equipment for naval, airborne and ground applications.

ENVIRONICS OY

P.O. box 349, fl-50101, Mikkeli, finland

+358-201-430-430 +358 201 430 441

sales@environics.fi

Timo Paakki, Samuli Kirjalainen, Ms. Katja Bengtsson, Mr. Tommi Kainulainen

Environics OY provides complete CBRN security solutions from early warning to consequence management. Environics also provides CBRN cleaning and decontamination products for crisis and consequence management.

EPE PROCESS FILTERS & ACCUMULATORS PVT LTD

Techni Towers, C-54/A, A.P.I.E, Balanagar, Hyderabad,

Andhra Pradesh - 500037

+91-40- 23778803 +91-40-23871447

business@epe-india.com

Mr. Narender Gauri, Managing Director Manufacture hydraulic accumulators in bladder, Diaphragm and Piston types, hydraulic and Process filters, filter Elements and spares for EPE and various other makes.

ERA A.S

Tprumyslova 387, 530 03 Pardubice, Czech Republic

+420-467 004 253 +420-466 670 461

http://www.erabeyondradar.com

era@era.cz

Era company is a pioneer and leading supplier of next generation surveillance and flight tracking solutions for the air traffic control, military, homeland security and airport operations markets.

EUC TECH

70 Ioid No 28, 4th Main Road, Cit Nagar, Chennai - 600 035

+91 44 42065044 +91 44243567

sales@euctech.com

Mr. S. Aravindhan, Marketing Manager +919790962633

EUC Tech's primary activity is in sales and support of OPEN MIND TECHNOLOGIES' hyper Mill product which addresses the requirements for quality programming for geometrically sensitive machinable components viz., impeller, structural parts, turbine blades, standard parts etc.

EUROCOTER

Aeroport Tarseiue/Provence

+331494344504

cecile.lion-lantuit@eoropter.com

Fovret Nelhzlie

The Franco-German-Spanish Eurocopter group is a Division of

EADS, a world leader in aerospace, defence and related services. Eurocopter offers the largest civil and military helicopter range in the world.

ELTA SYSTEMS LTD

Israel Aerospace Industries Ltd Liaison

D-4/5, Vasant Vihar,

New Delhi 110057, India

Telephone; 91 11 26143103/04, 26149788

Fax: 91 11 2614305, 26140177

E-mail: mail@iainewdelhicom (office)

ELTA Systems Ltd operates as a Defence Systems House, based on Electromagnetic Sensors (Radar, Electronic Warfare and Communication) and on IT. Its products include ISR Systems and Sensors, Early Warning Control, Communications, Defence and Self Protection, Target Acquisition and Fire Control.

EADS N.V.

Leiden 2303Da Netherlands,

P.O.Box 32008

+31 7152 45600

www.eads.com

press@eads.net

PTI Building, 3rd Floor,

4, Parliament Street,

New Delhi -110001,

P: 91-11-43579003,

Email: stefan.billep@eadsindia.com

The group includes airbus as the leading manufacture of comment and also tanker, transport and mission aircraft, Eurocopter as the world's large helicopter supplier and EADs astrium the European leader in suppliers programmes from Aarine to Galileo.

EID

Rajaji Marg, New Delhi-11

nepsols@gmail.com

Ramesh Dhar

EID is one of the leading high-tech industries in the field of command and control and defence communications.

ELBIT SYSTEMS GROUP

Elbit Systems Ltd., Advanced Technology Centre P.O.B. 539, Haifa 31053 Israel Tel: 972-4-8315315,

Fax: 972-4-855002

Elbit systems is a "multi-domestic" company engaged in a wide range of defense-related programs throughout the world, in the areas of aerospace, land and Naval systems, command, control, communications, computers and intelligence, surveillance and reconnaissance (c4isr), Electro-optics, security and services.

EMERSON CONNECTIVITY SOLUTIONS

7-13 Russell Way Chelmsford UK

+44 1245 342060 +44 1245 358938

connectivityeurope@emerson.com

David Hazell, Managing Director

Emerson Network Power Connectivity Solutions is the name behind Midwest Microwave, stratos international, Vitelec, semflex, Johnson and trompeter Electronics. A leading manufacturer of RF Microwave and fiber optic connectors, cable assemblies and Microwave Passive components and Devices.

FINCANTIERI

Via Genova 1 34121 Trieste Italy

+390403193111 +390403192427

pr@fincantieri.it

Antonini Corrado, Chairman; De Benedictis Massimo, Area Manager; Marchesan Daniele, Event Director

Fincantieri Cantieri Navali Italiani S.P.A., world leader in the cruise ships and large ferries sector. The company has to its core business: ships repairs and conversions, marine systems and components and mega-yachts.

FINMECCANICA SPA BERETTA

Piazza Monte Grappa, 4, 00195 Roma, Italy

+39-06-324731 +39-06-3208621

webeditor@finmeccanica.it

Samanta Crucioli, Head of Exhibitions & Events

202, Eros Corporate Tower,

Nehru Place, New Delhi-110019,

P:91-11-46545500

Email:giuliano.enea@finmaeccanica.com

Finmeccanica is the largest Italian industrial group in high technology and is one of the largest aerospace, defense and security players in the world.

FUTURA AUTOMATION PVT LTD

S4, Off 3rd Cross, 1st Stage, Peenya Industrial Estate, Bangalore-560058

91-80-28375290/28375293

91-80-28375291

www.futuraautomation.com

gganesh@futuraautomation.com

G. Ganeshr

FUTURA AUTOMATION has been into design and manufacture of rugged computers and displays.

GE AVIATION

One Neumann Way, Cincinnati, Oh 45215, USA

+1 513 243 2000

sales@euctech.com

Reddi Ramaswamy, Director, GE Aviation Programs, Military Systems Business – GE Aviation, Airport Road A-1, Golden Enclave, Bangalore,

GE Aviation, an operating unit of the General Electric Company, is a world-leading provider of jet engines, components and integrated systems for commercial and military aircraft. GE aviation also has a global service network to support these offerings.

GENERAL DYNAMICS UK LTD

11-12 Buckingham Gate, London Sw1e 6lb, United Kingdom

+44 (0) 20 7932 3400

+44 (0) 20 7932 3401

www.generaldynamics.uk.com

andrew.boyle@generaldynamics.uk.com

It's C4i technology meets the requirement of the battlefield Management System (BMS); it's leading technical solutions offer critical national infrastructure (CNI) protection from the threats; its expertise in producing shelters and its capability at integrating equipment legacy or new-makes it makes him one leading prime systems integrators.

GEOMINE LTD

Michmanim 20106, Israel

972-4-99882047 972-4-99882047

www.geomineisr.com

avi@geomineisr.com

'Geomine Ltd. concerns,itself with deciphering aerial photographs and locating landmines via remote sensing.

GEETA ENGINEERING WORKS PVT. LTD. & M/S. N. N. SHIPBUILDERS AND ENGINEERS PTE LTD

216, Devashree Garden Commercial Complex, R.W. Sawant Road, Majiwada, Thane - 400601

+91-22-21721122, 21721150

+91-22-21721446

www.geetaengineering.in

geeta.engg@rediffmail.com

GEW is specialized in Design, Development, and Manufacture of ship's Equipment :

i. Electro-hydraulic steering gears with VME 64 based controls.
ii. Rudder & rudder stocks.
iii. Propeller & stern gear (F.P & C.P.P.)
iv. All kinds of Deck Machineries.

GOA SHIPYARD LTD

Vaddem, Vasco Da Gama,

Goa - 403802

0832 2512152 to 2512156

0832-2513260

contactus@goashipyard.com

S. S. Bhat, General Manager (Technical Services)

Goa Shipyard Limited (GSL) the product range includes Patrol Vessels, special Purpose Warships, survey Vessels, landing crafts, fast attack crafts, sail training ships, Offshore supply Vessels, high speed interceptor boats, tugs, etc.

GODREJ AND MERLO

Godrej Material Handling, Godrej & Boyce Mfg. Co. Ltd., Plant 16, Pirojshanagar, Vikhroli,

Mumbai - 400079

+91 22 6796 4660 +91 22 6796 1519

mhemktg@godrej.com

Neville Wankadia, Dy.General Manager; Dattaprasad Khedkar, Associate Manager; Sumeet Bansal, Associate Manager; Dheeraj Saxena, Deputy Manager

Godrej Material handling is the largest manufacturer of material handling equipment in India. In partnership with crown, Komatsu, Merlo and hubtex .

GRINTEK EWATION(PTY) LTD

13 De Havillannd Crescent, Persequor Technopark, Pretorion, RSA

+27124216214 +27124216216

markting@ewation.co.za

Grintek Ewation is a system engineering company engaged in the design and production of sophisticated communication monitoring, direction finding, countermeasures, spectrum management and integrated security systems.

GRINTEX INDIA LTD

7th Floor, Left Wing, JMD Pacific Square, Near 32nd Milestone, Sector 15-II, Gurgaon, Haryana - 122201, India.

0091 124 4652400 0091 124 4652421

info@grintex.com

Mr Hariharan Gautam, Director; Radm N P Gupta, CEO- Naval & Maritime System Division

A leading high end technology and systems company provide system integration and technical support for Defense, Aviation, Space and Commercial Segments.

GTR&PC ZORYA-MASHPROEKT

Prospekt Oktyabrsky 42a, Nikolaev 54018, Ukraine

+380 512 49 76 48

+380 512 49 76 48

spe@mashproekt.nikolaev.ua

Mr. Vladimir Plugnikov, Advertising Specialist

They produce marine gas turbines with rated power 3, 6, 10, 16 and 25 MW as well as gearboxes and completed COGAG, COGAS and CODOG propulsion plants for all kind of ships, hovercrafts and hydrofoils.

GUMARNY ZUBRI, A. S

Hamerska 8 756 54 Zubri,

Czech Republic

(+420) 571 662 463

(+420) 571 662 299

www.guzu.cz

jana.havranova@guzu.cz

The company has experience in development, production and sale of:

- civil and military protective gas masks
- special isolation protective suits
- moulded technical rubber
- extruded rubber and plastic products for automotive and non-automotive industries
- rubber compounds

GARMIN CORPORATION

1200 E. 151 st Street, Olathe, KS 66062-3426 (Kansas City metro area)

(913) 397-8200, Fax: (913) 397-8282 www.Garmin.com

Garmin Corporation engages in the design, manufacture, and marketing of navigation and communications electronics products such as Global Positioning System Navigator, Integrated Cockpits, Panel mount Displays, Multi-function Displays, Transponders, Radar and other related Avionics.

GOODRICH CORPORATION

14/1 & 15/1, Maruthi Industrial Estate-Phase II, Hoody, Whitefield Road, Bangalore 560048

Mr Chris Rao, Director Aircraft Interior Products

Goodrich Corporation is a global supplier of systems and services to the Aerospace, Defence and Homeland Security Markets. The company product include Aero structures, Actuation Systems, Landing Gear, Aircraft Interior Products, Safety Systems, Aircrafts Wheels & Brakes etc

GENERAL DYNAMICS

Suite 1907, Shangri-La Hotel, 19, Ashoka Road, New Delhi -110 001

+91 11 41191907/08 +91 11 41196900

sbhattacharjee@india.gd-ic.com

Dr. Fredrick Axelgard, Director-International Business Development.

General Dynamics is a market leader in business aviation; land and expeditionary combat vehicles and systems, armaments, and munitions; shipbuilding and marine systems; and mission-critical information systems and technologies. General Dynamics has four main business segments. Aerospace designs, develops, manufacturers and services a comprehensive offering of advanced business-jet aircraft.

GREAVES COTTON LTD

Industry Manor, Appasaheb Marathe Marg, Prabhadevi, Mumbai-25

022-24397625 022-24377730

rrao@greavesmail.com

Mr. Rajiv Kulshreshta, Regional Manager (Northern Region; Mr. M.J.S.Walia, Vice President (Automotive Division); Mr. V. Sridhar, Vice President (Agro Equipment Division); Mr. V.D.Sivakumar General Manager (Auxiliary Power Division)

GSC GLASS PVT. LTD.

Plot 5 & 7, Udyog Vihar Industrial Area, Greater Noida- 201306

Uttar Pradesh, India

0120 2569922 0120- 2569288

gsc@gscglass.com

Mr. Vijay Kumar Chaudhry-G.M. (Automotive Sales)

GSC Glass Pvt. Ltd. is one of the leading glass processors in India. The company manufactures variety of energy saving glasses and provides total glazing solution.

GE INTELLIGENTS PLATFORMS

SeaFire AW manufacturer all weather, long range tracking System and Cobra dedicated operator. An electro optical tracking system optimised for deployment in land based scenarios that require a high performance solution which is also rugged and compact.

HARRIS CORPORATION

1680 University Avenue, Rochester, New York,14610, USA

1 585 241 8189 585241893

nignatow@harris.com

Charles Spyra, Regional, Director

+44 118 964 8022; Kevin Hardiy, Major Account Manager 44 7919 4246

Harris RF communications is the leading global supplier of secure radio communications and embedded high-grade encryption solutions for military, government and commercial organizations.

HELLENIC DEFENCE SYSTEMS SA

1 Ilioupoleos Ave., 172 36 Hymettus, Athens, Greece

+302109799201 +302109799205

ammosales@eas.gr

Michael Daskalakis, Ammunition Sales & Marketing Director

Eas's Defence sector operates 5 modern factory complexes for the production of infantry Weapons, Mortars, Weapon and Missile systems, ammunition of small, Medium and large caliber and External Payloads for aircrafts.

HINDUSTAN AERONAUTICS LTD

Corporate Offic E, 15/1 Cubbon Road, Bangalore - 560 001

080-22865197 080-22867140

www.hal-india.com

marketing@hal-india.com

Dr. Jayekar Vedamanickam, General Manager - Marketing

Hindustan Aeronautics Limited (HAL), is south East asia's largest aeronautical industry with proven capabilities in R&D, manufacturing and maintenance of fighters, trainers, transport aircraft, helicopters, their engines, accessories (hydraulics, pneumatic, fuel aggregates and instruments), avionic systems (radars, navigation system, communication system etc.) and associated systems.

HUTA STALOWA WOLA S.A.

1 Kwiatkowskiego Str.37-450 Stalowa Wola Poland

+48 15 813-73-40 +48 15 813-49-84

www.hsw.pl

cpw@hsw.pl

HUTA STALOWA WOLA S.A. - manufacturer and exporter of artillery systems 20-155mm, mortars, armoured vehicles and engineering equipment.

HALBIT AVIONICS PVT LTD

Hal Airport Departure Lane, Hal Estate, Vimanapura P.O.,

Bangalore - 560017

080-40491000

080-41605000/40491040

contact@halbit.co.in

Gp. Capt (Retd) Pradeep N. Srivastava, CEO; Mr. Hagai Raz,

CTO & VP-Business Development; Mr. Vinay Kumar C.R, Manager - SW & Visual

Halbit Avionics is a joint venture of Hindustan Aeronautics Ltd. India and Elbit System Ltd. Israel. It provides state of the art infrastructure, lab and hanger for the final integration of simulators and anionics integration & assembly. Avionics and large display solution Halbit Avionics has established capability for advance large display solution (LDS).

HGH SYSTEMS INFRAROUGES

Zac De La Sablière, 10 Rue Maryse Bastié 91430 Igny France

(33) 1 69 35 47 70 (33) 1 69 35 47 80

http://www.hgh.fr/

hgh@hgh.fr

High Infrared Systems design, develop, assemble and sell complete optronic systems for security, industrial and civil applications.

HI-TECH ROBOTIC SYSTEMZ LTD

B13, Infocity Ph. 1, Sector 33/34, Gurgaon, Haryana, India - 122001

01244715300 1244715398

marketing@hitechroboticsystemz.com

K. Srinivasan, Vice President; Prashant Joshi, Head Marketing

Hi-tech robotics systemz is mobile robotics and artificial intelligence company.

HM ARZENÁL ZRT

+36/42 210-801 +36/42 210-802

www.hmarzenal.hu

info@hmarzenal.hu

Modernization and repair of radars, repair of MAVERICK missiles head and production of safety and security systems.

HONEYWELL

1944 E. Sky Harber Circle,

Phoenix, Az 85034

602 365 2665 602 365 2075

http://www.honeywell.com/aero

alan.n.robinson@honeywell.com

Alan N Robinson,

Trade Show & Special Events Manager

4th Floor, Nirlac House, B 25 Qutab Institutional Area, New Delhi-110016,

p: 91-11-42399900,

Email:shyam.uttamsingh@honeywell.com

Honeywell is a world leader of high-technology solutions for defense and space customers. From precision guidance targeting components to fully integrated civilian and military systems that power unmanned vehicles.

HYPRECISION HYDRAULIK

34, Sanjay Building No.6, Mittal Industrial Estate, Andheri Kurla Road, Andheri (East), Mumbai - 400059

91-22-28502960/2850 8283

(91-22)2850 1284

hhpl@bom3.vsnl.net.in

Gourav Rajani

PRODUCTS DESIGNERS & MANUFACTURERS Turnkey Electro-hydraulic systems,hydraulic cylinders, telescopic cylinders fabricators of special Purpose Plc/ hydraulic Mobile Equipments, Deck machineries Winches/ Windlass/ capstans Boat Davits,Test rigs/ flushing & filtration Machines, Hydraulic hoist for gates etc.

IAI ISRAEL AEROSPACE INDUSTRIES LTD

Ben Gurion International, Airport

972-3-9353567 972-3-9355933

avbahar@iai.co.il

D-4/5, Vasant Vihar,

New Delhi-110057,

P: 91 11 2643103/04,

Eamil: jbhasin@iainewdelhi.com

Israel Aerospace Industries (IAI) is a globally recognized leader in defense and civil aerospace technology.

IDEAFORGE TECHNOLOGY PVT LTD

Office No. 4, 4th Floor, Kresit Business Incubator, IIT Bombay, Powai, Mumbai 400076

+91 22 2572 1122 +91 22 2572 1220

Info@Ideaforge.Co.In

Amardeep Singh, VP - Marketing & Operations

Ideaforge is focused on design, development and manufacturing of man-portable unmanned aerial systems.

INDIAN ARMOURED VEHICLES

Universal Lane, Dudhola

Palwal 121102, Haryana, India

01275-2622000 01275-262148

sales@iavpl.com

Mr. Anil Kant, CEO

Products Range:-

Vehicle armouring, Weaving of Kevlar, Concealable armour, Ballistic shield etc.

INDUSTEEL - ARCELOR MITTAL GROUP

Industeel France - Etablissement Du Creusot, 56 Rue Clemenceau, 71202 Le Creusot Cedex, France

33-03-85805555 33-03-38805500

www.industeel.info

Subsidiary of ARCELOR MITTAL group, Industeel has expertise in the production of high quality special steel plates and prefabricated products for industrial equipment.

INFRARED SECURITY SOLUTIONS

Foxhall Lodge, Foxhall Road, Nottingham, Mg7 6LH United Kingdom

+44 (0) 115 845 6573

+44 (0) 115 845 6574

sales@iss-tc.com

Steve Shepperd, Director +44 (0) 7799 545381; John Matthews, Director

+44 (0) 7879 697466

Infrared Security Solutions (ISS) specialises in the design and supply of sensors and systems that provide 24 hour vision. Used for fugitive search, intruder detection, VIP protection as well as border, perimeter and costal surveillance.

INTEL DESIGN SYSTEMS INDIA PVT LTD

47, Industrial Estate,

Lonavla - 410401, Pune, India

+91-2114-272681 +91-2114-273465

idslnl@gmail.com

S.D Vartak, Managing Director

Intel Design Systems (I) Pvt. Ltd. is approved manufacturer and supplier of Electronic, Electromechanical equipment and systems for tanks, Automatic fire Detection and suppression systems for AFV, NBC Detection and Protection systems for AFVs, shelters.

ISRAEL WEAPON INDUSTRIES (IWI) LTD

Bialik 64 Ramat Hasharon

Israel 47100

972-3-7606000 972-3-7606001

karinae@israel-weapon.com

Gil Wainman

The company's weapon systems include the innovative TAVOR family of assault rifles, the ultimate two caliber x 95 (assault Rifle & SMG), the reliable NEGEV LMG, the well-known GALIL assault rifle family.

IVCHENKO-RPOGRESS

2, Ivanova Str., Zaporozhye, 69068, Ukraine

380 612 650327 380 612 650327

progress@ivchenko-progress.com

The sphere of its activities covers design, manufacture, certification, overhaul, test, development and putting into series production and further improvement of consumer's characteristics of gas turbine engines of aircraft and industrial applications.

IXSEA

53 Ubi Ave 1#03-10 Paya Ubi Industrial Park Singapore 408934

+65 6747 4912 +65 6747 4913

www.ixsea.com

info@ixsea.com

Muhamed Ali

IXSEA: experts in navigation and positioning systems for marine and land forces.

IRKUT CORPORATION PRODUCT & DETAILS

Bldg. 1, 68, Leningradsky prospect Moscow, 125315, Russia

Phone/fax: (+7 495) 777-21-01

inbox@irkut.com

Irkut Corporation conceives designs, builds, deploys, and supports top-of-the-line aircraft. Its products include: Su-30MK Multirole Combat Aircraft, Civil Airplanes, Multipurpose Unmanned Aerial System, Combat Navigation and Targeting Systems, Civil Airplanes, etc.

ICX TECHNOLOGIES

ICX Technologies is a leader in the development and integration of advanced sensor technologies for critical facility protection.

INNOVATIVE CLAD SOLUTIONS PVT LTD

H-2, Suneja Chambers, 2nd Floor, Alaknanda Comml. Complex,

New Delhi-19, India

011-26027174 011-26026776

djssandhu@shivalikbimetals.com

Dr. Brijendra Jha; Mr. D.J.S Sandhu 9811047467; Mr. Kabir Ghumman 98930-00320

Innovative clad solutions are into manufacturing of various combinations of clad Metals/strips. apart from applications in heat Exchangers, cable shielding, battery, cookware, coinage, bearing products, etc., clad Products are also used in Defence applications, such as bullet Jackets / cups, etc.

INSTASOL TECHNOLOGY PVT LTD

Donald House, 1st Floor, Opp. Electric House, Colaba Causeway,

Mumbai, 400001, India

98600-25000/98200-45035

(022) 66459096

india@instasol.com

Sachinsuri Director 98600-25000, Sumeetsuri CEO

The product portfolio of instasol focuses on highly sophisticated technologies in following areas:

- Directed Energy Weapons
- Bomb Disposal, Containment and Storage Systems
- Border Surveillance Systems
- Oil & Gas Field Security Systems.
- Bird Detection and Deterrent Systems
- Hovercrafts & Airboats

ITL OPTRONICS LTD

11 Granit St., P.O.Box 10168, Petach Tikva 49002, Israel

972-3-9277444 972-3-9277445

www.itloptronics.com

itl@itlasers.com

Eli Venezia, President & CEO; Yishai Akerman, Marketing & Business Development: India

ITL'S comprehensive and advanced electrooptical product families and land system solutions (hardware and software) include:

- Night Vision systems - image-intensified and Thermal imaging
- Weapon sights, fire control systems and laser aiming lights
- Observation and target acquisition systems
- Laser rangefinders and OEM modules

ITT

1650 Tysons Blvd, Suite 1700, Mc Lean, Va 22101, USA, S-3 1st and 2nd Floor, Green Park Extension,

New Delhi - 110016

12604514250 18183661078

www.itt.com

evelyn.teichner@itt.com

Ron Smith, VP Business Development, India +91 (11) 4602 8681

ITT provides communications, sensing and surveillance, space solutions, advanced engineering and integrated services, and a wide range of products for aircraft systems for government and commercial customers.

JAHAGIRDAR AERO PRODUCTS

204/A Station Road, Ahmednagar 414001 (Mh) India 91 241 2355023,

91 98220 54630 91 241 2328810

japaero_anr@bsnl.in

Y. P. Jahagirdar, Yash Jahagirdar

Designers and system integrators of aerial targets unmanned aerial Vehicles remotely Piloted Vehicles unmanned airships Precision guided aerial Delivery systems.

JENA-OPTRONIK GMBH

Prussingstrabe 41, 07745 Jena, Germany

+493641200202 +493641200222

ulf.krause@jena-optronik.de

Ulf Krause-Director, Defence and Security Instruments; Thomas Roedar, Director Sales-Defence and Security Instruments; K.Skandamurugan, Director Marketing-Authorised Indian Representative

Jenoptik subsidiary Jena-Optronik GmbH (Division Defense and Civil Systems) develops, manufactures and markets opto-electronic instruments and systems for various applications in the area of aerospace, intelligence and reconnaissance.

JETAVI ENGINEERING PVT LTD

348/349 Brooklands, 13th Main, Sadashivnagar, Bangalore - 560080

12604514250 18183661078

www.itt.com

padma@aeronics.in

Evelyn Teichner, Trade Show Manager +1 260 451 4250; Ron Smith, VP Business Development, India

+91 (11) 4602 8681

HEICO Corporation manufacturer of approved jet engine and aircraft component replacement parts, other than the original equipment manufacturers (OEMs), and their subcontractors.

KÄRCHER FUTURETECH GMBH

Max-Eyth-Str. 35, 71364 Winnenden, Germany

+49 7195 14 0 +49 7195 14 2780

www.wew.de

futuretech@de.kaercher.com

Jens Bauer, Managing Director; Dirk Waldow, Area Sales Manager

Kärcher Futuretech GmbH develops, manufactures, and markets products for:

NBC Protection Systems,NBC Protective Clothing,

Application-oriented high-pressure steam cleaners.

KIGRE, INC

100 Marshland Road,

Hilton Head Island, Sc 29926 USA

011-843-681-5800 011-843-681-4559

jeffmyers@hargray.com

Michael J. Myers, President

Kigre has invested in the development of solid-state laser materials and technologies.

KINECO PVT LTD

60, Pilerne Industrial Estate, Pilerne Bardez Goa-403 511 0832-6648888 0832-6648889

pankaj@kinecogroup.com

Pankaj Naik, Sr. Engg Projects and Marketing

Kineco Private limited is a company based in Goa, India manufacturing tailor made composite products for a wide range business sectors like aerospace, Defence, Mass-transit, automotive etc.

KINTEX SHAREHOLDING COMPANY

66, James Baucher Blvd., 1407 - Sofia, Bulgaria

(+359-2) 8662311 (+359-2) 9631123

minkin@mbox.contact.bg

Mr. Javor Stoykov, Senior Commercial Officer

The company is fully owned by the state and has basic activities in the sphere of:

• Armament, ammunition, Unmanned aerial Vehicles, Optical sights and binoculars, Communication and electronic warfare means, radar equipment.

KONGSBERG DEFENCE & AEROSPACE

P.O box 1003, Kongsberg 3601 Norway

+4732288200 +4732288620

office.kda@kongsberg.com

Svein kjonigsen, Director Marketing Coordination

KONGSBERG DEFENCE & AEROSPACE is the leading Norwegian defence contractor. The defence activities focus on Missiles and communications.

KONTRON TECHNOLOGY INDIA PVT LTD

425, 3rd Floor 2nd Main Road, Kasthurinagar, East of NGEF, Bangalore - 560043

+91 (0) 40972761 +91 (0) 42277127

http://www.kontron.com

salesindia@kontron.in

Mr. Nijesh Parmar, Chief Operating Officer; Mr. Janardhan Prabhakar, Business Development Manager

Kontron designs and manufactures embedded and communications standards-based, rugged COTS and custom solutions for OEMs, Ystems integrators, and application providers in a variety of markets.

KRASNY MARINE SERVICES PVT LTD

1201/1202, Great Eastern Summit, 'B', 12th Floor, Plot No. 66, Sector - 15. CBD Belapur, Navi Mumbai - 400614

022-27563425 022-27563414

krasny@giasbm01.vsnl.net.in

Cdr. V.G. Jayaprakasan, Managing Director;

Certified by the CEMILAC for undertaking repairs of Russian origin military avionics. Company has promoted Rosoboronservice (India) and Avrora (India) as Indo-Russian Joint Ventures.

KRISHAN BROTHERS

4651, Bazar Ajmeri Gate,

Delhi - 110 006

011 2321 1490 011 2685 4740

www.krishanbrothers.com

kbros@vsnl.com

Krishan Kumar Agarwal

Sole Distributor in India for Precision Tools for Automotive, Aviation, Electrical, Electronics, Engineering, Plant Maintenance, Telecommunication etc. Advanced Clamping Devices for Welding, CNC Machines, Wood working and Metal cutting snips etc.

KVH INDUSTRIES, INC

50 Enterprise Center, Middletown, Rhode Island, 02842 USA

1-401-847-3327 1-401-849-0045

http://kvh.com/fiberopt/

info@kvh.com

Christine Marion, Sales Manager, Guidance & Stabilization 401-845-8126; Jay Napoli, Vice President, FOG & OEM Sales 401-487-6689

Manufacturer of solutions that provide global high-speed internet, television and voice services via satellite to mobile users at sea, on land, and in the air.

KADET DEFENCE SYSTEMS

25/1 Rowland Road, Kolkata 700 020, India

+91 33 2486 3904/+91 98300 67989 +91 33 2485 0249

ceo@kadet-uav.com

Avdhesh Khaitan, Maj Gen; J S Mahil, AVSM (Retd), Chief Mentor and Strategic Advisor- Military Sales

A specialized unmanned systems company designing, manufacturing and operating unmanned aerial systems for intelligence, surveillance and reconnaissance (ISR) purposes for use by the military and special forces.

KAMAN PRECISION PRODUCTS

217 Smith Street, Middletown,

CT 06457 USA

1-860-632-4536 1-860-632-4536

fuzing@kaman.com

Mr. Ken Kelly, Director - Business Development; Mr. Stephen Cardy, Business Development Executive; Mr. David Oliveria, Business Development

Manufacture of safing and arming solutions for the ordnance and other industries.

KIRLOSKAR GROUP

Hadapsar Industrial Estate,

Pune - 411 013/ India

+91 (20) 2672 7000 +91(20)2672 7508

deshpandepramod@kpcl.net

Mr. Pramod Deshpande, Vice President (Corporate Marketing)

Currently offers the following products to the Indian Armed Forces: Army:

- Power packs for armored vehicles like MBT'S, ICV'S, etc.
- All terrain Vehicles
- Trolley mounted/skid mounted/ mobile containerized Diesel generating sets

- Hydro-pneumatic suspension for main battle tank
- Mobile high pressure compressor for missile launcher
- Nitrogen generators for artillery guns

Air force:

- Service air trolley for Military aircraft (for cooling cockpits)
- Mobile air charging vehicles for aircraft maintenance
- Mobile airfield high pressure compressors
- unified gas service stations for aircrafts

KOMMLABS DEZIGN PVT LTD

A - 46, Sector - 4, Noida

0120 40900 00 +0120 40900 01

info@kommlabs.com

Mr. Shailesh Saxena, Manager - Business Development; Mr. Amit Sharma, Assistant Manager - Business Development; Ms Surbhi Kakkar, Marketing Coordinator

Kommlabs provides interception solutions to intelligence agencies, law enforcement agencies and communication service Providers.

KOREA AEROSPACE INDUSTRIES

8255-851-1314 8255-851-0835

pjijc@koreaaero.com

Jongin Park

As a sole company to design, manufacture and integrate aircraft in the Republic of Korea, Kai produces t-50 advanced Jet trainer, Kt-1/ Ka-1 basic trainer, UAV and has been developing 429 helicopter. Kai is developing the KhP (Korean helicopter Program) as the integrator of KhP and is participating in space business.

LARCET SRL

Via luigi biolchini

+39 06 40043894 +39 06 5573843

mcitro@larcet.com

Ms. Maria Francesca D'Angelo; Ms. Marisa Citro, Marketing and International Sales

Larcet SRL is an Italian company specialized in Designing, Producing and Marketing of Power supplies; ac-dc/dc-ac/ac-ac/dc/dc for any Kind of application, in Particular for Military and civil applications.

LPS BOSSARD PVT LTD

NH10, Delhi Rohtak Road, Kharawar by Pass, Rohtak - 124001

+91 1262 305199, 305161

+91 1262 305111, 305184

defence@lpsboi.com

Have a range of more than 60,000 of fasteners in Stainless Steel, High Tensile Steel, MS, Brass, Copper, Aluminum, Titanium Alloy, Inconel and Plastics and Multifunctional fasteners like, Self Drilling Screw, Thread Cutting, Thread Forming Screws, EcoSyn, EcoFix .

LUFTHANSA

56, Alps Building, 1st Flr, Janpath, New Delhi 110001,

Tel: 23724200

Deutsche Lufthansa AG is one of the Largest Airlines in Europe. The company has its focus on its five business areas: Passenger traffic, Logistics, MRO, Catering and IT services.

LUCENT TECHNOLOGIES

3rd Floor, NSE Building, Exchange Plaza, Bandra Kurla Complex Bandra (E) Mumbai- 400051 India

Tel: +91-22-56798700

Fax: +91-22-26598542

Lucent Technologies India Ltd DLF City 15th Floor, DLF City-I, Gurgaon, Haryana 122001

T: 0124 2560366

Lucent designs and delivers the systems, software, solutions and services for next generation communications networks for services providers and enterprises. Its business units include: Integrated Network Solutions (INS), Mobility Solutions, Lucent Worldwide Services (LWS).

LAGGAR INDUSTRIES

Sobti Nagar, VPO Nurpur, Pathankot Road, NH, Jalandhar, Punjab

91 181 6537621,2,3,4 91 181 2611840

Devendra Dwivedi, Vice President

91 9811692025

"LAGGAR INDUSTRIES" specializes in bullet proof steel and later introduced commercial production for bullet proofing of vehicles and for manufacturing of other security products.

LASER DEVICES INC.

70 Garden Court, Monterey,

Ca 93940

(831) 373-0701 ext: 233 831 333 9230

rader@laserdevices.com

Richard Ader

Laser Devices engineer and manufacture sophisticated electro-optical devices from concept design through completion using the latest technology and custom made parts.

LAVERSAB INDIA

2145, 17th Main, 2nd Cross, Indiranagar, Hal II Stage,

Bangalore - 560008

+91 94484 83702, +91 93412 28107

www.laversab.com

naveen@laversab.com,

shankar@laversab.com

Laversab India Sells, services and supports RVSM compliant automated Pitot static testers air Data test sets and air Data calibrators to customers in the commercial, Military and corporate aviation markets.

LOCKHEED MARTIN INDIA PVT LTD

Room 152, Taj Palace Hotel, Sardar Patel Marg, Diplomatic Enclave, New Delhi 110 021

66116510 66303553

promila.pinto@lmco.com

Sean Hanrahan, Business Development Analysis Director 301-897-6438

Headquartered in Bethesda, MD, lockheed Martin is principally engaged in the research, design, development, manufacture, integration and sustainment of advanced technology systems, products and services.

LARSEN & TOUBRO LTD

Gulab Bhawan, New Delhi, India

011 41509978, 011 4150 9979

bhatiaajay@larsentoubro.com

MAHINDRA DEFENSE SYSTEMS (DEFENCE LAND SYSTEMS)

Mahindra Towers 1st Floor, 2A Bhikaji Cama Palace,

New Delhi, 110066

011 - 41220349 011 - 41458505/510

pandit.satyendra@mahindra.com

Brig(Retd) K A Hai,

Director 9810005536;

Defence land systems India (DLSI) is a joint venture enterprise between Mahindra & Mahindra Ltd (M&M) and BAE systems plc. Mahindra Defence systems, M&M Division, is one of the leaders in armouring of light vehicles in India.

MARINE FORCE INTERNATIONAL LLP

8 Waterloo Place, Sw1y 4be London, United Kigdom

+442079253200 +442079253201

mfi-info@marineforce.net

Mr. Anoop Govil, Genral Manager

MarineForce International LLP (MFI), has the tasks and responsibilities for the submarineyards of thyssenKrupp Marine Systems AG:

MARLOG MARINE LOGISTIK

Warftstress 179, 24142 Kiel/Germany

+4943170500 +494317050121

info@mariog.de

Mr. Anoop Govil, Genral Manager

MARLOG, subsidiary of Howaldtswerke-Deutsche Werft GmbH and Man Ferrostaal AG is available for supply of spare parts, consultancy, technical assistance, refresher training, infrastructure and shore based facilities.

METALTECH MOTOR BODIES PVT LTD

Plot No.68, Sector 3, IMT Manesar, Gurgaon 122050

0124-4369272 0124-4369271

swthatte@metaltechmotors.com

Shri J B Sehrawat, Managing Director

Designers, developers and fabricators of customized solutions on prime movers for Police, Para Military forces and Defence services in bullet proof and Non bullet proof segment.

MILSYS (UK) LTD

Ramsden Road, Rotherwas Ind Est, Hereford, Hr2 6Np, UK.

+44 1432 277197 +44 1432 277375

info@milsys.co.uk

Steve Babbage, Business Development

Milsys (UK) Ltd is a provider of mobile infrastructure capabilities and solutions for defence, security and crisis relief organisations.

MILTECH HELLAS SA

90 I. Metaxa Str, 19400 Karellas, Attica, Greece.

+302106647320 +302106647322

miltech@miltech.gr

Konstantinos Koutsos, CEO & Managing Director

The company specializes in projects and products to satisfy the needs of the international Defense industry in the areas of:

- Aerospace & Avionics Electronics
- Cables & Harnesses
- Tactical Communications Equipment
- Electro-optics, Electronic fuses, Modernization Programs

MOTOR SICH, JSC.

15, 8th of March Str., Zaporozhye, 69068, Ukraine

380 061 7205000 380 061 7205000

motor@motorsich.com

Motor Sich JSC is one of the world's largest companies in the field of manufacture, aftersales support and overhaul of 55 types and modifications of up-to-date and dependable engines for various fixed-wing and rotor-wing aircraft.

MS INSTRUMENTS PLC

Unit 4, Ravensquay Business Centre, Cray Avenue, Orpington, Kent Br5 4bq.

+44 (0) 1689 883020

+44 (0) 1689 871392

pauleverington@msinstruments.co.uk

Paul Everington, Managing Director

MS Instruments Plc (MSI) is an advanced technology company whose major activities are in design and manufacture of ballistics instrumentation & live fire training system as well as specialized security systems.

MAINI PRECISION PRODUCTS PVT LTD

5-A Bommasandra Industrial Area Bommasandra, Bangalore -560099

40724700 7833505

pselvaraj@mainimail.com

Maini Global Aerospace Pvt Ltd (MGA) Bangalore, a fully owned subsidy of Maini Precision Products Pvt Ltd.

MAXTECH NETWORKS

Maxtech Networks is a pioneer and leading provider of ad-hoc wireless mobile networks, for manufacturing of solutions for resilient.

MBDA

1 Avenue Reaumur, F-92358 Le Plessis Robinson Cedex

33(0)1 71 54 17 69

33(0)1 71 54 00 31

christine.merlet@mbda-systems.com

Ms Christine Merlet

MBDA is a world leading missile systems company with a comprehensive product range designed to meet the land, naval and airborne guided Weapon system requirements of each of the armed forces.

MEMORY ELECTRONICS PVT LTD

1119-1120 Naurang House, KG Marg, New Delhi-110001

91 11 30424957 91 11 30424556

Maj Gen (Retd) SV Thapliyal,

Vice President, Business Development

91 9899855132

Memory Electronics is engaged in the manufacture and supply of Radio & Satellite communication systems Optronics and Electro Optronic systems simulators Electronic fuses Early Warning Systems etc.

MKU PVT LTD

13, Gandhi Gram, Kanpur-208007. UP. India

+91 512 3026700 +91 512 3026799

protection@mku.com

Ganesh Athley, GM Sales (India)

MKU offers certified solutions for defence applications, its products include:

- Personal Protection
- Helmets, Ballistic Over-vests, Up-armor inserts, Anti-Mine suits etc.
- Vehicle Protection
- Light Weight armor solutions for vehicles, Platform armoring for helicopter and Naval Vessels
- UAVS
- Night Vision Devices

MORPHO DETECTION

+91 9845130160 +91 80 28528329

pravin.surana@morphodetection.com

Pravin Surana, S.Asia Region Business Manager

Sagem Sécurité's Morpho Detection, inc. (MD) a business of the safraN group is a leading supplier of explosives and narcotics detection systems.

MEGGITT TRAINING SYSTEM, INC

296 Brogdon Road, Suwannee, Georgia

+1 678 288 1090 +1 678 288 1513

peter.stammers@megggitt.com,

ajaygupta.srg@gmail.com

Peter Stammers, Vice President Business Development Asia/ Pacific Region

Meggitt Training Systems Inc. design, manufacture virtual training systems providing training in the handling and use of small and supporting arms for military and law-enforcement customers.

MISHRA DHATU NIGAM LIMITED (MIDHANI)

Hyderabad India

mktg_4@yahoo.com,

kpsmk27@yahoo.co.in,

hanumantharao.midhani@ap.nic.in, devjitghosh@gmail.com

Satpal Singh, General Manager 919871286514 PA

MOOG QUICKSET[JANUS-INDIA]

G-13, Unitech, South City Gurgaon-122001 India

91 124 4086641/42 91 124 4086640

www.janustradingco.com

technical@supersleuth.co.in

Ashish Satpathy 91 9971941121

NIGHTLINE, INC

300 Industrial Drive, Mountain City, TN 37683 USA

011-423-727-5900 011-727-6948

r.smith@nightline.us

Russell Smith, Sr. Vice President

Nightline is a US owned and operated company providing night vision systems, laser devices and tactical equipment to military and law enforcement personnel.

NIGHTSEARCHER LTD

Unit 4, Applied House, Fitzherbert Spur, Farlington, Po6 1TT, Hampshire, Portsmouth, United Kingdom

+44 23 9238 9774 +44 23 9238 9788

andrew.s@nightsearcher.co.uk

Andrew Sanczuk,

Export Sales Manager

Nightsearcher ltd is manufacturer of portable rechargeable lighting products for professional applications. Product range includes high quality and carefully selected area lights, scene lights, floodlights, searchlights, hand-lamps, flashlights and head-torches.

NOBLE AEROSPACE PVT LTD

307, 3rd Floor, Raja House, 30-31, Nehru Place, New Delhi - 110019

011 41617246 011 41617271

business@noblefix.com

Adarsh Shishoo, CEO & Director

Key products are : Helicoil Repair Kits, Helicoil Inserts, Helicoil Taps and Toolings, "Aviation Specific - Helicoil Oversize & Twincoil Repair Kits, Helicoil Range Kits", Key thread inserts, Dodge Brass Inserts, Plastic Inserts, Threaded Inserts, thread profile cutting taps.

NORTHROP GRUMMAN PRODUCT & DETAILS

Suite 1517, The Shangri - La,

19, Ashoka Road

New Delhi - 110 001, India

P: 91-11-41196917 F: 91-11-41191517

E: gyanendra.sharma@ngc-india.com

Cmde Gyanendra Sharma, (Retd.) Managing Director (India)

Northrop Grumman Corporation Integrated Systems

Northrop Grumman Corporation provides innovative systems, products, and solutions in information and services, electronics, aerospace and shipbuilding. Products: Airborne Tanker Transport, Space Craft, Space Radar, Long-range Strike Aircraft Bomber, Cruiser and Advanced Wireless Broadband Systems.

NATIONAL INSTRUMENTS

Bangalore Office: 81/1 & 82/1, Salarpuria Softzone, Wing B, 5th Floor, Block A Bellandur, Varthur Hobli, Bangalore 560103, Karnataka, Delhi Office: 311&312, rectangle - 1, D-4, District Centre, Saket,

New Delhi - 110017

080-41190000, 011-42658282

ni.india@ni.com

Rajeev Krishnan, Strategic Sales Manager

National instruments or Ni (www.ni.com) help design, prototype and deploy systems for measurement, automation and embedded applications.

NIDUS ENTERPRISES PVT LTD

75, Dharmdev Nagar, Isanpur, Ahmedabad, Gujarat 382443

079 30221291 079 25710214

tarak@climbingworld.com

Nirat Bhatt, Chairman; Tarak Patel, Managing Director; Reema Rey, Director

Supplier of tactical and outdoor gear like rope, harness, ascending and descending gear, climbing gear, breaching tools, tactical eyewear, tactical clothing, tactical lights, extreme cold clothing, footwear, climbing wall etc.

OMNIPOL A. S.

Nekazanka 11 112 21 Praha

Czech Republic

(+420) 224 011 111 (+420) 224 012 241 www.omnipol.com

omnipol@omnipol.cz

- Export of Defence and Security Equipment:
- tracked and wheeled armoured and

  engineering vehicles
- simulation systems and training devices
- Nbc detection, protection and

  decontamination equipment
- surveillance, reconnaissance and monitoring systems
- stock spare parts for T-55, T-72 and BVPS

ORBIT TECHNOLOGY GROUP

8D Hatzoran St. Netanya,

Israel 42504

+972 9 8922771 +972 9 8922801

Group@Orbit-Ltd.Co.Il

Naomi Azrieli, Marcom Manager; Prince Dallal,

Sales and Marketing director

Orbit is a leading designer, developer and manufacturer of innovative secure Digital audio communication systems for a wide range of military and commercial applications.

OTO MELARA SPA

Via Valdilocchi N. 15, 19136 La Spezia, Italy

+39 0187 583395 +39 0187 582795

marina.magnani@otomelara.it

Marina Magnani,

Marketing/Communication

OTO Melara, a company of finmeccanica group, is a world leader in design and production of small and medium calibre naval guns, with research and development capabilities ranging from naval guns to conventional and intelligent ammunition, from artillery to turrets, from missile launchers to airborne armament.

OFFSET INDIA SOLUTIONS

208 Pragati House, 47-48 Nehru Place, New Delhi 110019, India

+91-11-3263-7474 +91-11-2621-9022

info@offsetindiasolutions.com

Mr. Sanjay Bhandari, Chairman & MD

Offset India Solutions (OIS) is a unique advisory and consulting organization that provides expertise to international companies of repute for success in their initiatives to fulfill Offset obligations throughout its lifecycle.

OXLEY GROUP LTD

Priory Park, Ulverston, Cumbria, LA12 9QG.

+44(0) 1229 582621

+44(0)1229 581851

sales@oxleygroup.com

Andy Bednarek,

Sales & Marketing Director

JVE Oxley specialize in the design and manufacture of advanced high quality electronic and electro-optic components and systems for aerospace and defence platforms.

PEARSON ENGINEERING

Wincomblee Road, Walker, Newacstle Upon Tyne, England

+44 191 2340001 +44 191 2620402

pearson@pearson-eng.com

Mr. Randall Flack, Technical Director; Mike Jordan, Sales Manager

Pearson Engineering Ltd specialise in the design and manufacture of combat engineer equipment and the modification of existing vehicles to provide an armoured engineer capability.

PLASAN

Mp Merom Hagalil 13870, Israel

+972 4 680 9000 +972 4 680 9001

www.plasan.com

noamh@plasan.com

Mr Noam Hen, Vice President, International Sales & Marketing

Plasan is an international company engaged in the design, development, and manufacture of state-of-the-art, lightweight, ballistic armor protection products and integrated survivability systems.

POLICSKE STROJIRNY

572 12 Policka, Czech Republic

420- 461 751 100 420- 461 751 105

military@pos.cz

The company at the present time, is certified for the demilitarization and environmentally friendly disposal of all types of ammunition with expired periods of warranty and of unexploded ammunition found in the field.

PULSE INTECO LTD

Ner Ha-Layla 13b Ramat Poleg, Netanya, Israel 42209

+972-9-8353129

+972-9-8353177

pulse@techpul.com

Mr. Samuel Weiner, CEO

The company is involved in research, development, design and manufacturing in the fields of laser physics, optics, electronics and mechanics, with the emphasis placed on tube thermal imaging systems.

PCI LTD

ushagambhir@prime-pci.com

Usha Gambhir 9999028042

PCI limited is the distributor for FLIR Systems. FLIR is the world leader in providing high performance stabilized gimbal Electro Optical systems as well as light weight thermal sensors for hand held applications and weapon mounted thermal sights.

PENTAGON RUGGED SYSTEMS

11-5-397/1, 5th Floor, Fortune Manzil, "Pentagon Block", Hyderabad 500004

91 40 23300495, 23301261

91 40 23300496

http://www.prsindia.co.in

jrthomas@prsindia.co.in

JR Thomas, Manager - Business Development 995 995 2877

Specialized in the following areas:

- Checkout systems
- Fire control systems
- Obc systems
- Un-manned ground vehicle (ugV)
- Off-rout mining
- Battle field surveillance sensing systems

PIPAVAV SHIPYARD LIMITED

Skil House, 209 Bank Street Cross Lane, Fort, Mumbai 400023

91-22-66199171 91-22-226966023

rmbhatia1@gmail.com; contact@pipavavshipyard.com

Mr Nikhil P Gandhi, Group Chairman

Pipavav Shipyard Ltd (PSL) is having an excellent infrastructure designed to meet the global shipbuilding standards. The modern state of art steer cutting, welding, bending machines and panel lines used at Psl coupled with modern shipbuilding procedures of international standards makes it an ideal platform for the construction of warships including submarines in addition to commercial ships & Offshore Platforms. It's dry dock is the India's largest dry dock, 662m x 65m, services by two largest goliath cranes, each of 600 tons capacity.

PRECISION OPERATIONS SYSTEMS (INDIA) PVT LTD

Commodore Malhotra 91 9811915473

Precision Operations Systems (India) Pvt. Ltd. provides equipment for Bomb Detection and Disposal, blast inhibitors, blast containment Vehicles, radio Monitoring and surveillance, Direction finding and location fixing, Night Vision and thermal imaging Devices.

PUNJ LLOYD LTD

78, Institutional Area,

Sector 32, Gurgaon

0124-2620123 0124-2620111

deveshdwivedi@punjlloyd.com

Mr. Aditya Vit, Group President Defence; Col. (Retd) Anddrew A Fernandes, Group VP, Defence; Mr Aditya K Shrivastava

Punj Lloyd Group provides integrated design, engineering, procurement, construction and project management services in

a) Manufacture, assembly, Maintenance and Overhaul of weapons and land systems

b) Maintenance and Overhaul of aircraft
c) Design and engineering capability

PARAMAHANSA TECHNOLOGIES LTD

A 602, Ansal Chambers 1, Bhikaji Cama Place, New Delhi - 110066

+91 11 46584992 +91 11 46584993

pramodvothayoth@yahoo.co.in

Pramod V Othayoth, Director

Authorised vendor and sole distributor for 'CG Kinetic Cutters' made by the swedish "Carl Gustav" under the SAAB Dynamics which can be used for both rescue/recovery and tactical purpose. Are also the authorized vendor for the Swedish "Act Safe" for their 'powered ascenders" and the US company "Stidd Inc" for their submersible vehicles.

RAYTHEON

2000 East El Segundo Blvd., El Segundo, Ca 90245, USA

1-310-6478606 1-310-6470734

kmpatton@raytheon.com

Walter F. Doran, President, Raytheon International, Inc., Asia; Mr. A K Mathur Country Manager, Raytheon International, Inc., India

Raytheon provides state of the art electronics, mission systems integration and other capabilities in the areas of sensing; effects; and command, control, communications and intelligence systems, as well as broad range of mission support services.

RAYTHEON COMPANY

Suite 198, Hyatt Regency, Bhikaiji Cama Place, Ring Road, New Delhi - 110066

91 11 2671 6314 +91 98 101 91876

a_k_mathur@raytheon.com

Admiral Walter F. Doran, President, Raytheon International; A K Mathur, Country Manager

Raytheon provides state-of-the-art electronics, mission systems integration and other capabilities in the areas of sensing; effects; and command, control, communications and intelligence systems, as well as a broad range of mission support services.

REAL TRADE PRAHA A.S

Starokosirska 3/695, Praha, Czech Republic

+420 775 708 281 +420 469 775 113

doshkov@realtrade.cz

Mr. Petr Kratochvil, Mr. Petr Rusek, Mr. Lyubomir Doshkov, Mr. Jan Stralka

Real Trade Praha A.S. was established as a trading company dealing with military hardware and spare parts for t-72, t-55, BMP-1 and others. At present the company is authorized to trade with a wide spectrum of military sortiment including arms, weapons, big caliber arms, ammunitions, bombs, missiles, tank technics, aircrafts, helicopters and all spare parts for the mentioned technics.

REUTECH COMMUNICATIONS

34 Kings Road, Pinetown, 3610, Kwazulu-Natal, South Africa

+27 31 719 5700 +27 31 719 5800

www.reutechcomms.co.za

communications@reutech.co.za

Johan Volschenk

Reutech Communications specializes in technologically advanced secure V/

UHF Communication Systems for use on airborne, naval and land based platforms

RHEINMETALL AG, CORPORATE SECTOR DEFENCE

Rheinmetall Platz 1, 40476 Dusseldorf, Germany

+49-211-473-01 +49-211-473-4729

info@rheinmetall-defence.com

The Taj Mahal Hotel. Office Suite 422, Number One, Mansingh Road, New Delhi- 110011,

P: 91-11-23026060

Rheinmetall Defence's core competencies stand for capabilities-oriented innovation: new generations of vehicles with optimized protection concepts, network-enabled sensors and optronics, platform-independent turrets and weapon systems, C-RAM-capable air defence, and high-performance ammunition including propellants.

RIPPEL EFFECT

Po Box 12434, Hatfield,

South Africa, 0028

+27-12-809-3469 +27-12-809-3470

www.rippeleffect.com

charl@rippeleffect.co.za

Mr. Petr Kratochvil, Mr. Petr Rusek,

Mr. Lyubomir Doshkov,

Mr. Jan Stralka

Rippel Effect Systems (PTY) Ltd is the manufacturer and supplier of the world's only qualified fourth generation 40mm multi-shot grenade launcher systems.

ROCKWELL COLLINS

400 Collins Road Ne, Cedar Rapids, Iowa 52498 USA

1.319.295.1000, 1.319.295.1649

learnmore@rockwellcollins.com

T C Chan, Vice President and Managing Director, Asia Pacific; MKR Prasad, Managing Director; Alan Jahn, Director, Asia Pacific Government Sales

Plot No S-3, 1st & 2nd floor, Green Park Extension, New Delhi-110016

Tele : 91 11 46028684,

Email: skmishra@rockwellcollines.com

Rockwell Collins is a pioneer in the design, production and support of innovative solutions for customers in aerospace and defense. Expertise in flight deck avionics, mission communications, information management, and simulation and training.

ROHDE & SCHWARZ INDIA PVT LTD

A-27, 1st Floor, Mohan Co-Operative Industrial Estate, Mathura Road,

New Delhi 110 044

+91 11 425354-00 +91 11 425354-33

www.rohde-schwarz.co.in

sales.rsindia@rohde-schwarz.com

ROHDE & SCHWARZ supplies powerful, interoperable communications systems, trunked radio (TETRA) and encryption.

ROXEL PROPULUIOS SYSTEM

Centre D'affaires La Boursidière - Immeuble Jura – 92357 Le Plessis-Robinson Cedex - France

+33 (0) 1 41 07 82 82

+33 (0) 1 41 07 82 03

www.roxelgroup.com

ROXEL GROUP is mastering the whole of the activities relating to propulsion for tactical weapons and for tactical cruise missiles.

ROLLS ROYCE GROUP PIC

Birla Tower West, 2nd Floor, 25, Barakhamba Rd, New Delhi 110 001

91-11-23357120, 23357118

F: 91-11 23357117

E: anil.shrikhande@rolls-royce.com

Mr Anil Shrikhande President, Rolls-Royce India Ltd

Rolls-Royce is a British Aircraft Engine Maker. It provides Power Systems and Services for use on land, at sea and in the air. Products include: Euro Fighter Typhoon, Joint Strike Fighter F-35 Aircraft, C 130J Hercules, Phantom F4K &F4M, Propulsion Systems, Submarine Equipment etc.

RADA ELECTRONIC INDUSTRIES

7 Giborei Israel St., P.O.Box 8606 Netanya 42504 Israel

+972 9 8921111 +972 9 885885

eelan.hight@rada.com

Herzle Bodinger, Maj. General (Res.) President & Chairman; David Mayer, Marketing Director

RADA Electronic Industries Ltd. is a Defense Electronics system house specializing in sophisticated, military-oriented electronic systems for airborne and land applications.

RADIALL INDIA PVT LTD

Radiall India Pvt Ltd, 25D, IInd Phase, Peenya Ind Area,

Bangalore - 560058

080-28395271/39220094

080- 28397228

www.radiall.com

infoin@radiall.com;

kunal.kapoor@radiall.com

Radiall supplies a broad range of high reliability interconnect products meeting the complex technical specifications of multi-signal, RF and fiber optic interconnect connector technology.

RAFAEL ADVANCED DEFENSE SYSTEMS LTD

P.O. Box 2250 (190) Haifa,

Israel 31021

+972-4-879-4717 +972-4-879-4657

intl-mkt@rafael.co.il

Flat no. 505, Silver Arch Apartments, 22 Flroz Shah Road,

New Delhi-110001, India,

P: 91-11-41504036/7/8/9

Rafael provides state-of-the-art, systems and weapons in the fields of Missiles, air defense, naval systems, target acquisition, EW, C4ISR, communication networks, data links, electro-optic payloads, add-on armor, combat vehicle upgrading, mine field breaching, border and coastal protection systems, breaching munitions.

RAHMAN INDUSTRIES LTD

184/167, Wajidpur, Jajmau,

Kanpur, India

91 512 2462118 91 512 2465357

www.rahman-group.com

tehreem@rahman-group.com

Mohd. Tehreem Razwi,

COO 91 9650296117, 91 9810936413

RAHMAN INDUSTRIES LTD. is an ISO 9001-2000 company and manufacturers of safety/ security footwear.

RENAULT TRUCKS DEFENSE COMMUNICATION

5bis, Allée Des Marronniers -

Sat Ter 2 40 - Cs 30502- 78008 Versailles Cedex - France

www.renault-trucks-defense.com

anne-claude.buatois@renault-trucks.com

Specialized in all aspects of road haulage, renault trucks designs, produces and sells global road transport solutions worldwide. With its comprehensive range of vehicles (from 2 to 60 t)

RENEWABLE ENERGY SYSTEMS LTD

D-13, Ida, Phase-V, Jeedimetla, Hyderabad-500055, A.P., India

+91-40-23097279 +91-40-23097279

resph5@hotmail.com

P.Suryanarayana,Director;Lt.Col.(Retd)

K.V.S.Ramarao, EXECUTIVE; T.V.L. Narasimharao, EXECUTIVE

Renewable Energy Systems Ltd., (RES) is the manufacturer of thermal batteries based on various electro chemistry.

ROLTA INDIA LTD

Tower A, Rolta Technology Park, Midc, Andheri (E) Mumbai.

91 22 29266666 91 22 28365992

roltacorp@roita.com

Lt. Gen Pps Bhandari, Director Operations

Rolta provides innovative solutions in Enterprise geospatial information solutions (EGIS), Defense and homeland security; Enterprise Design and Operations solutions (EDOs); and Enterprise Information Technology Solutions (EITS).

RONOGIL MANAGEMENT & SERVICES PVT LTD

Lgf, C-55, NDSE-1,

New Delhi-110049

+91-11-46052711 +91-11-46052712

info@ronogil.com

Mr. Atul Gupta, (Manager- Business Development (Defence)

+91 9811 636929; Mr. Ronen Hermoni, CEO +972 5 4569 6081

Thales communications inc., USA and its products are represented in India through Ronogil Management and Services Pvt. Ltd.

ROTAX ELECTRONICES PVT LTD

12, Shaheed Bhagat Singh Marg, New Delhi -110001

+91 11 23746506/23361779

+91 11 23344174

rotaxele@de13.vsnl .net.in

Mr. Surindar K. Gupta, Managing

The company represents large number of leading foreign manufacturers in the field of bomb Detection and Disposal such as: NIJD Super Broom / Super Broom Plus, Bomb Suits with Cooling System, Telescopic Manipulator, Neutrex Waterjet Disrupter MK –II, Surveillance and Anti Sabotage Equipment etc.

SB ENGINEERS

404, Ornet Arcade, Opp. Simandhar Tower, Off. Satya Marg, Bodakdev, Ahmedabad -380 054, Gujarat, India.

079 2685 4375 079 2685 4345

sbengineers@sbgroupindia.com

Mr. Keyur Shah, CEO

SB Engineers are the exclusive agents for the new MIRICLE range of high resolution miniature ruggedised thermal imaging cameras.

SCANNA MSC LTD

223 Regent Street, London, Wib21b, United Kingdom

+44 207355355 +44 2073553556

info@scanna-msc.com

Jason Pett, Sales Manager

SCANNA MSC is a leading UK manufacturer of compact and portable screening and detection equipment.

SCD - SEMI CONDUCTOR DEVICES

P.O.Box 2250 Haifa, 31021 Israel

972-4-9902535/2500

972-4-9902627/2686

www.scd.co.il

marketing@scd.co.il

Semi conductor Devices (SCD) develops and manufactures a full spectrum of cooled and uncooled infrared detectors and laser diodes.

SCHLEIFRING UND APPARATEBAU GMBH

Am Hardtanger 10,

82256 Fuerstenfeldbruck

+49 8141 4030 +49 8141 40345

sales@schleifring.de

Romesh Kumar Singhal, Managing Director

Covers all sectors of the requirement for leading edge electrical slip ring systems and non-contacting high data rate rotary joints for the military industries.

SELEX GALILEO

Christopher Martin Road, Basildon, Essex Ss14 3El UK

+44 1268 522822 +44 1268 885232

Mino Manekshaw, Regional Business Development Manager (India)

+91 (0) 99105 57 105

202 Eros Corporate Tower,

Nehru Place, New Delhi-110019

SELEX Galileo, a Finmeccanica company, is a leader in the defense electronic markets, with a distinctive strength in airborne mission critical systems and a wide range of capabilities for the battlefield and homeland security applications.

SELEX COMMUNICATIONS

Via Pieragostini, 80 16 163,

Genova, Italy

39-010-614-7267 39-010-885706

enrica.falcon@selex-comms.com

SELEX Communications, a Finmeccanica company, is a global supplier of advanced communication, navigation and identification solutions to protect communities and critical national infrastructure.

SERIAL INNOVATIONS INDIA PVT LTD (SIIPL)

1,17th Main, 4th B-Blk,100 Ft Road Koramangala, Bengaluru -560034

91-80-41999555 91-80-41999777

info@sitpl.com

Mr. Girish Kachroo, NSM, Ankit Kumar, TM, Tim Mitchell, Managing Director, Arvind Lakshmikuamr, COO

SITPL develops state of the art solutions in security and safety, for defence, civil forces, and industry the company has competencies in algorithms, real-time system software and hardware, electronics and vision systems.

SFTE SPETSTECHNOEXPORT

7, Moskowsky Avenue,

Êiev, 04073, Ukràinå

+38-044-5685072/5685051

+38-044-5685062

dc1@ste.kiev.ua

Mr Petro Fedorchuk, Chief of Department

- Repair, modernization, warranty and after warranty maintenance of all types/ of Mig Aircraft, TU-142M, IL-38, SU-25, -27 AND MI- 8, MI-17, MI-25/35, KA- 25, KA-28 Helicopters;
- Overhaul of R-13, 25, 29, RD-33 AND AI-31F

Aero Engines, KSA-2

SFTE SpetsTechnoExport is capable to offer for supply of all kind of spares and raw materials for different types of armored vehicles, tanks and artillery systems of Russian and Ukrainian origin.

SIDERVAL SPA

Via Roma, 39/C, 1-23018 Talamona, Sondrio, Italy

+39-0342-674111 +39-0342-670400

www.siderval.it

siderval@siderval.it

Tiziano Luzzi, Sales Area Coordinator

One of the leading specialist manufacturers in the world of special hot extruded steel shapes.

SIKA INTERPLANT SYSTEMS LTD

3, Dr. Sharma Building,Gangadhar Chetty Road, Bangalore - 560 042, India

+91 80 25599144 +91 80 25599501

sales.ae@sikaglobal.com

Rajeev Sikka, Chairman & Managing Director

SIKA Interplant Systems Ltd, specialise in systems, products and engineering services for the aerospace and defence industries, the company will showcase pioneering.

SKL (INDIA) PVT LTD

2117-c, Oberoi Garden Estates, Chandivali, Andheri (East),

Mumbai 400072

022 28476652 022 28476649

sklmumbai@rediffmail.com

Mr. K M Bhatia, Managing Director; Mr. Ravi Bhatia, Director

Products and services offered are:

1. Air Cooled Diesel Engines and Genset from MOTORENFABRIK HATZ GMBH& CO. KG, Germany.
2. NBC DecontaminationSystems for Civil and Defence Application from Kaercher Futuretech GMBH, Germany.
3. Mil Grade Air Conditioning Systems for Shelter and Tent Applications from Zhendre S.A. France.

SPEECH TECHNOLOGY CENTER

4 Krasutskogo Street,

Saint Petersburg 196084, Russia

+7 812 331-0665 +7 812 327-9297

info@speechpro.com

Mr.Harsha Shetty,

International Sales Manager;

Software, equipment, training and technology creation in areas such as Voice recording, lawful interception, Noise cancellation and speech enhancement, forensic audio examination and analysis.

STOP STICK INTERNATIONAL, INC

365 Industrial Road Harrison,

Oh 45030, Contact in India,

SRG Techno (P) Ltd, 210, Bahu Plaza, Rail Head Complex Jammu, J&K 180012 India 513-202-5500,

+91 191 24706 06/07/08

+513-202-0240

rwilliams@stopstick.com

Robert M. Williams, Director of International Sales

Stop stick international inc. are the world leader in tire deflation devices that are used by law enforcement agencies.

STRATOS 07 S.R.O

Na Folimance 13 120 00 Praha 2 Czech Republic

+420 603 416 872 +420 312 658 151

straka@stratos07.cz

Mr. Josef Straka

Rescue Parachutes for gliders and experimental aircraft the MAGNUM product line for maximum weight of 2,3 tonne for the sport aircraft pilots Ju-40 for paragliding and hang-gliding Plus 25, 31, 34, 36, 48, 66 stratos 07 is also involved in the manufacturing of ballistic armor and riot protection for law enforcement personal and the aircraft.

SURE SAFETY

42 a/b, Yoginagar Township,

Chhanai Road, H no. 8,

Vododara-391750

+91 265 2760150 +91 265 2774824

generalmanager@suresafety.com

Mr. Nishith Dand, Director

For Defense Segment it provides the World's best Water / Air tight 'Pelican' Protector Cases which are rugged and used for housing any equipment requiring utmost protection from dust/ heat / water / vibration etc. 'Pelican' also provides flashlights (torches) with high luminosity using both lEDs and xenon bulbs.

SAAB AS

Hotel Le Meridien, Suite 1904, Windsor Place Janpath,

New Delhi - 110001

P: 91-11-23716989 F: 91-11-23716991

E: janwiderstrom@saab.se

Mr Jan Widerstrom Vice President

Svenska Aeroplan AB has long experience of building Advanced Aircraft, Command and Autonomous Weapon systems. Its products include: Electronic Warfare, UAVs, Sensor Systems, BMP 202, Tactical Support Systems, Logistics and Maintenance, etc.

SAFRAN

34, Poorvi Marg, Vasant Vihar,

New Delhi 110057

Tel 011-26156483/85

Fax: 011- 26156431

Email: snecmadelhi@vsnlcom

Mr S Kumar Business Development & Corporate Affairs Safran

Safran is a high-technology group, organized in four branches: Aerospace propulsion, Aircraft equipment. Defence Security and Communications.

SINGAPORE TECHNOLOGIES ENGINEERING LTD

41 A, Ground Floor, Kalu Sarai Sarvapriya Vihar

New Delhi 110016, India

(91) 11 41048411

Fax: (91) 11 41048410

(91) 981844 1807

Lt. Col (Retd) Harpal Singh Director, Marketing (South Asia)

Singapore Technologies Engineering Ltd's diverse commercial activities cater to the Aerospace, Electronics, Land systems and Marine sectors. Products include: Large-Scale Systems Group, Communication & Sensor Systems Group, Software Systems Group

SISTEMA

13 Mokhovaya Street,

Moscow 125 009

Tele : +7 (495) 737-01-01

Fax: +7 (495) 730-03-30

www.sistema.com

AFK Sistema develops and manages businesses in selected service-based industries, including telecommunications, technology, banking, real estate, retail and media. Its products include:

Microelectronics, Banking, IT & telecom, Retail, Media, Radar & space House building, Travel, etc.

SOLTAM SYSTEMS

Box 13 Yokneam, 20692, Israel

E-mail: info@israeli-weaponscom

Tel: 972 4 9896424

Fax 972 4 9892045, 972 54 4513687

E-mail: shane_c@soltamcom Website: www.soltam.com

LTC (res) Shane Cohen, Bsc Marketing & Sales Director PO

Soltam operates both on the Military market and the civilian market. Its military expertise is Artillery Systems, Cannons and Ammunition. Products include: Artillery, Mortars, Ammunition, etc.

S M CREATIVE ELECTRONICS LTD

10, Electronic City, Sector-18, Gurgaon-122015, Haryana, India

0124 2455203-205 0124-2455212

yeldo@smcel.com

Mr. Sanjay Trehan, Managing Director

Design, Development and Manufacturing of switch Mode Power conversion Products for Military & Nuclear applications.

SAGAX KFT.

Haller Utca 11-13, H-1096, Budapest

+36 1 219 54 55 +91-11-46052712

www.sagax.hu

info@sagax.hu

Sagax designs and manufactures, software defined and digital radio technology based products and offers services for electrical, signal, communication intelligence and electronic warfare.

SAGEM IS A HIGH-TECH COMPANY

Haller Utca 11-13, H-1096, Budapest

www.sagem-ds.com

Sagem is a high-tech company in the safran group. It is a world or European leader in solutions and services in optronics, avionics, electronics and critical software for the civilian and military markets.

SAMTEL

6th Floor, TDI Centre, District Centre - Jasola, New Delhi-110025.

+91.11.42424000 +91.11.42424099

puneet.kaura@samtelgroup.com

Mr. Puneet Kaura, Executive Director

Samtel straddles the entire value chain from design, development, manufacture, testing, qualification, repair and maintenance and obsolescence management of avionics products and Display systems for Military as well as Marine applications.

SDS ELECTRONICS PVT LTD

Plot No.194, Industrial Area,

Phase -II. Chandigarh

Mr. Yogeshwer Sahdev, Managing Director; Mr. Kuldeep Sahdev, Director

Integrate various security systems i.e

a) IP based CCTV surveillance system with inbuilt intelligence softwares viz. motion detector alarm, image identification and classification, intrusion detection, tail gating, image tracing, traffic density monitoring etc.
b) Electronic access control system
c) Personal and baggage screening system
d) Explosive Detection and Disposal systems

SERO LTD

+36 1 433 2181 +36 1 433 2182

www.sero.hu

info@sero.hu

Sero Ltd. is a Hungarian company specializing in military trading and production.

Main area of activity:

- Demilitarization of gun powders and explosives
- Sales and delivery of military equipment spare parts, ammunition
- Production of gepárd gM6 'lynx" aMr rifle
- Production of .308 and .338 sniper rifles

SERVOCONTROLS AEROSPACE INDIA PVT LTD

Survey No 683, Industrial Estate, Udyambag, Belgaum - 590008, Karnataka, India

0831 - 4219555, 2407501/2/3

0831 - 2484496

sales@servocontrolsindia.com

Mr. Deepak Dhadoti,

Managing Director

Servocontrols is the system house of closed loop controls for both hydraulics and Electromechanical controls. Servocontrols design, manufacture, assemble, test and install at site the various customs built servo Systems.

SHREE LALITA

7-C, Laxmi Industrial Premises,

New Link Road,

Andheri (W) Mumbai - 400053

91-22-67023356/57 91 22 67023358

shreelalita@vsnl.com

Mr.Harshil Lalaji, Vice President; 098201 57022;

Shree Lalita - providing a wide range of safety & rescue & disastermanagement products and consultancy services & specialised training.

SIG SAUER

18 Industrial Drive, Exeter, NH 03833

(603) 418-8168 (603) 773-2113

www.sigsauer.com,

Jacklyn.Jacobson@sigauer.com

Jacklyn (Fahlin) Jacobson, Events Manager

SIKORSKY AIRCRAFT CORPORATION

91 120 4320 966 91 120 4236 966

ajswalia@sikorskyasia.com

Sikorsky Aircraft Corporation is a world leader in the design, manufacture and service of military and commercial helicopters; fixed-wing reconnaissance aircraft; spare parts, maintenance, repair and overhaul services; and civil helicopter operations.

STEEL FORCE N.V

Lange Klarenstraat 16-20., B-2000, Antwerp, Belgium.

32 3 2034260 32 3 2034269

laurent.alloo@steelforce.net

Mr. Rakesh Sharma, Mr. Atul Vaidya, Mr. Laurent Alloo, Ms. Shalini Pandey

Steel Force N.V. is the sales and marketing partner of Ruukki (Finland) in India. Ruukki manufactures armor steel - RAMOR.

SYSTEM CONTROLS

73-B, Keonics Industrial Estate, Electronics City, Bangalore.

91-80-28522297/28523587

91-80-28523507

www.system-controls.com

marketing@system-controls.com

System controls is a System Solution Provider with the focus to serve Defence, R & D and aerospace market.

SHRI LAKSHMI DEFENCE SOLUTIONS LTD

19/X-1, Krishnapuram, G.T. Road, Kanpur - 208007, India

0512-2402893, 2402733

0512-2402339

anil@shrilakshmi.in

Anil Kumar Verma, Director; Abhishek Agarwal, President; Col (Retd) K R Bhatnagar; V.P. Technical, Col (Retd); Ravi Prasad, V P Marketing

Shri Lakshmi Defence Solutions Ltd. has a wide range of products from armored vehicles, combat uniform gears, Tactical gears, Body armors, Armoring solutions for Vehicle/ aviation/ Naval Industry, Helmets, Multi spectral camouflage nets etc.

SURE SAFETY SOLUTIONS PVT LTD

607 / 2 DDA Building, Tower II, District Centre, Janakpuri,

New Delhi - 110058 India

91 11 25554347 91 11 25554348

www.suresafety.in

info@suresafety.in

Sunil Khurana

SURYA TELECOM PVT. LTD

Sco 36, Sector 3,

Panchkula-134 112 India

0172-6573882

operahomes@gmail.com

Anil Sharma,

Manager (P&A) 9216223852

TAR IDEAL CONCEPTS LTD

5. Maavar Yabok St.Tel Aviv, Isarel

+972 3 6914564 03-6914567

iness@tarideal.com

Tomer Avnon, CEO; Omer Itzhaki, International Sales Manager

One Stop Shop focused on answering its clients' needs by providing a full package deal up to turnkey level, providing equipment and training in fields such as: riot and crowd control, K9, counter and anti terror, intelligence, ground-force, rappelling and others.

TEJAS NETWORKS LTD

58, 1st Main Road, J.P. Nagar,

3rd Phase, Bangalore -560078

91-80-41794600 91-80-41214481

info@tejasnetworks.com

Mnisha Gangey, VP–Business Development

Tejas pioneered the development of SDH/SONET as well as carrier Ethernet product that enable telecom carriers to converge traditinal voice based transmission networks with the new data dominated networks.

TELLUMAT (PTY) LTD

64-74 White Road, Retreat,

Cape Town, 7800, RSA

+27-0-21-710-2911

+27-0-21-710-2350

avionics@tellumat.com

Marc Anderson, Managing Executive: Defence

Tellumat Defence has business units, namely Radar, Sia Solutions, Identification and Tactical Communications. Competencies within Tellumat Defence include project management, system engineering, product development, industrialization, manufacturing, installation, commissioning, logistic support and quality assurance. The identification business supplies integrated IFF (identification friend or foe) integrator, transponder & cryptographic products and systems for land, airborne and naval use. The tactical communication business provides systems such as real-time, low latency analogue and encrypted digital data links for unmanned aerial vehicles (UAVS), fixed and rotary wing aircraft applications.

THEON SENSORS SA

57 I. Metaxa, 194 00 Koropi,

Athens, Greece

+302106641420 +302106644093

info@theon.com

Nikolaos Katsimitros, Ammunition Sales & Marketing Director

THEON Sensors specializes in the design, development, manufacture and integration of Electro-Optical sensor systems for defence and security applications.

THYSSENKRUPP MARINE SYSTEM

Herrmann-Blohm-Strasse 3,

Hamburg/Germany

+494018000 +494018001111

marisystems@thyssenkrupp.com

Mr. Anoop Govil, General Manager

ThyssenKrupp Marine system (TKMS) is one of the largest European shipyard groups. In the field of naval shipbuilding the company is one of the leading system providers for:

- Non-nuclear submarines
- frigates and corveters
- Mine wafare vessels
- Patrol boats and auxiliaries

TIP TOP GENERAL AGENCIES PVT LTD

80/1 block 2nd Whs, Kirti Nagar,

New Delhi 15

011-25153714 011-25153716

neha@rematipfopindia.com

Vineet Choudhari, Managing Director

Products and services mobility systems and services for bullet proof vehicles for VVIFs and other mine protected and security vehicles of defence and para military organizations.

TRUVELO MANUFACTURERS (PTY) LTD

Po Box 14189, Lytteiton 0140,

South Africa

+2711314-1405 +27112031848

marissa@truvelo.co.za

Mr. Ralf DH Gebert, Director

The company has established an unmatched name in the manufacture of barrels and highly accurate sniper rifles for long range shooting.

TULIP TELECOM LTD

C-160, Okhla Industrial Area,

Phase-1, New Delhi -110020.

011-66205000 011-41678002

sales@tulip.net

Sanjay Virnave, President Sales 9971699917;

B.K Devaya, National Manager Defence 9313309649

TULIP is at the forefront of Defence Communications. Network connectivity, secure, scalable bandwidth provisioning and management. Wired and wireless.

TYCO ELECTRONICS

Te Park Doddenakundi 2nd Phase Industrial Area White Field R.D Bangalore 560048

91-80-28540800 91-80-28540820

vidhyaiyer@tyconelectronics.com

Mr. Arun Simha, Country Manager

Tyco Electronics is a leading global provider of engineered electronic components.

TELEDYNE TECHNOLOGIES INC PRODUCT & DETAILS

1049 Camino Dos Rios

Thousand Oaks, CA 91360

Tele: (877) 666-6968

Website: www.teledyne.com

Teledyne Technologies Inc provides electronic components, instruments and communications products, including Defence Electronics, Data Acquisition and Communications Equipment for Airlines and Business Aircraft, Monitoring and Control Instruments.

TEXTRON

No 90 Madiwala, Hosur Road Bangalore - 560 068

P: 91-80-66939002 F: 91-80-67129088

E: nmohanty@textron.com

Mr N R Mohanty Chairman and Managing Director Textron India Private Limited, Textron Global Tech Centre Textron serves the General Aviation, Aerospace and Defence, Industrial and Commercial Finance Markets with products such as Vertical takeoff and landing aircraft, UAVs, light and mid-size business jets, utility turboprops, and single engine piston aircraft.

TASER INTERNATIONAL

17800 N. 85th Street, Scottsdale,

AZ 85255, United States

http://myces.bdmetrics.com/cdt-6277923/taser-international/details.aspx

TASER International is a company providing advanced Electronic control Devices and innovative secured digital evidence collection and management solutions for use in the law enforcement, medical, military, corrections, professional security, and personal safety markets.

TEIJIN ARAMID GMBH

Ballistic Protection Department, Kasinostrasse 19-21, D-42097 Wuppertal, Germany

+49-202-322354 +49-202-322351

www.teijinaramid.com

ballistics@teijinaramid.com

Teijin Aramid, leading supplier of aramid fibers under the brand Twaron®. Twaron is used throughout the world in ballistic protection.

TENCATE

4910 Old Jonesboro Road.

Building 500, Suit 501-A, Union City, GA

1 770-317 8097 1 678 658 8032

j.pezzini@tencate.com

Juliana Pezzini, Marketing Manager

TENCATE DEFENDER™ M is the flame resistant (FR) military combat fabric. Engineered with patented technology, TENCATE DEFENDER™ provides exceptional protection from flame and heat and is comfortable and durable for ground troops' daily wear.

TITAGARH WAGONS LTD

143, Indian Globe Chambers, Gr. Flr, W. H. Marg, Fort,

Mumbai -01 022-22673301

022-22691340

bombay@titagarh.biz

M. P. Sajeev, Associate Vice President

Titagarh Wagons Ltd. (TWL) is the largest freight Wagon builder for the Indian Railways. Developed the 'rail Mobile launch Platform' for the Agni Missile Programme. TWl is currently executing bulk orders for MBWT tank carrying wagons, integrated field shelters (CBRNE Collective Protection shelters), bailey bridges etc.

TATA GROUP

2nd Flr, Bombay House, Homi Mody Street, Mumbai-400001 India

91 22 6665 7579

mmoghe@tata.com

Mr Sanjay Singh 9223595235

Tata Companies Operate in seven business sectors: communications and information technology, engineering, materials, services, energy, consumer products and chemicals. In the recent past Tata Companies have made contributions to the integrated guided Missile Development Programme through work on the akash air force launcher and the Pinaka rocket system. The group has partnered the defence forces in the areas of command and control, battle management software, secure communications and rugged consoles.

UNIVERSAL FLEXIBLES PVT LTD

2C, Dyasandra Industrial Area,

4th Cross, White Field Roa Road, Mahadevapura P.O,

Bangalore - 560048

+ 91 80 - 28510878/28510122/ 43580305. 91 80 43580331

info@universalflexibles.com

Mr Venkatesh S Aiyer, Director Universal Flexibles Pvt. Ltd manufactures top of the line quality Hydraulic Hose Assemblies, SS Corrugated hose assemblies, hose fittings, adapters and tube assemblies.

UNITED TECHNOLOGIES CORPORATION

Centre, No. 21, Nehru Place,

New Delhi-110019

Phone +91-11-51207513

United Technologies Corp researches, develops and manufactures high-technology products including Aircraft Engines, Helicopters, Heating and Cooling, Fuel Cells, Elevators and Escalators, Fire and Security, Building Systems, and Industrial products among others.

VOUGHT AIRCRAFT INDUSTRIES

Lynne M. Warne, 615-974-6003

Email -warnely@voughtaircraft.com

Vought offers a full range of aero structures fabrication and assembly capabilities that are best suited for the design and manufacture of Fuselage Panels, Empennage and Flight Control Surfaces, Nacelles, Wings, Doors, Centre Wing Sections, Horizontal Stabilizers.

VOP 025 NOVY JICIN S. P.

Dukelská 102 742 42 Šenov U Nového Jièína, Czech Republic

(+420) 556 783 111

(+420) 556 701 734

www.vop025.cz

marketing@vop025.cz

VOP 025 is the state-owned company specialised in the repairs, modernization and reconstruction of wheeled and tracked vehicles.

VORTEX ENGINEERING WORKS

B-3, Phase -II, MIDC, Sagaon, Dombivli-East, Thane-421204, Maharashtra, India

+91-251-2871339, 6571451, 6574451 +91-251-2870044

www.vortex-clutch.com

sales@vortex-clutch.com

Abhilash. A.Walavalkar, Chief Executive

VORTEX is a leading manufacturer and exporter of Electromagnetic & hydraulic applied and released clutches and brakes for a wide range of industrial and vehicular applications.

VANTAGE INTEGRATED SECURITY SOLUTIONS (P) LTD.

B-11, Sector 7 Noida, Gautam Budh Nagar-201301, Uttar Pradesh, India 0120-4632200 (30 lines)

0120-4346883

info@vantagesecurity.com

Mr. Parmod K Verma- Managing Director; Mr. Pranav Verma- Executive Director

Vantage security is the manufacturer, distributor and system integrator of electronic security and surveillance products in India.

VECTRA

A-54 Kailash Colony,

New Delhi 110048, India

+91-11-43171111 +91-11-29235033

www.vectragroup.com

The core businesses of the group are aviation, engineering, material handling and construction equipment, automotive, real estate, information technology, and the services sector.Vectra has been able to expand its operations through partnerships with other global leaders such as Eurocopter of France, Orad of Israel and Kamaz Inc. of Russia.

WALLOP DEFENCE SYSTEMS LTD

Craydown Lane, Middle Wallop, Hampshire, So20 8Dx, UK

+44 (0)1264 783800

+44 (0)1264 783869

enquiries@wallopdefence.com

John Taylor, Managing Director

Wallop Defence Systems, a Division of Esterline Defense technologies, has years of experience and expertise in military pyrotechnics having been actively engaged in research, development and production of a wide range of advanced pyrotechnic devices.

WASS

Via Di levante

+390586840463 +390586854058

rosa.ricciardi@wass.it

Responsible for the design, development, production, integration and marketing:

- Heavy Weight torpedoes
- Light Weight torpedoes:
- Torpedo countermeasures for submarine and surface ships

WAPMERR INDIA

26 C/1 Khijrabad, New Friends Colony, New Delhi - 110 065

011-26323500 011-26323501

rajneesh_singh@wapmerr.in

Mr. Ishfaq Mir, Mr. Iqbal Butt, Mr. Lokesh Chopra, Mr. Jaewoog Yoo WAPMERR-India,one of the leaders in the development of innovative geo-information technologies using 3D-Modeling, navigation coupled with high end security and surveillance systems.

YEOMAN MARINE PVT LTD

29, 30, 31 & 33 Neelgiri Industrial Estate, T.J. Road, Sewri (W). Mumbai, 400 015 India.

+91 22 2410 0234 +91 22 2418 3988

info@yeomanmarine.com

Dhananjay Mishra Managing Director +91 9820082867

Yeoman Marine Pvt Ltd is a management company whose service arm is Yeoman Marine services, involved in ship and submarine repair and shipbuilding.

ZEVETA AMMUNITION A.S.

Tovarni 532, 687 71 Bojkovice,

Czech Republic

420-5-72612182 420-572 641 426

ammunition@zeveta.cz

ZEVETA manufacturing programme focused on the pyrotechnical production programme that is divided into three main parts:

- Development and production of various pyrotechnical products
- comprehensive testing of pyrotechnical products
- Ecological disposal and delaboration of ammunition Production programme

ZEN TECHNOLOGIES LTD

S 237 Ground Floor,

Greater Kailash-I, New Delhi-110048

www.zentechnologies.com

shefali.c@zentechnologies.com

Ms Shefali Chibber, Manager Mktg, 9871777093

Zen technologies limited, is a specialist training simulator company. The core competencies in, software, mechanical design, and interface electronics, electrical and pneumatic systems are integrated to meet the training needs of Military forces.

KH
2001

References

1. E. Anders Eriksson et all., "Study on the Effects of Offsets on Development of a European Defence Industry And Market, European Defence Agency.
2. Laxman Kumar Behera, "India's Defence Offset Policy 2008", *IDSA Comment*, August 19, 2008.
3. Laxman Kumar Behera, "India's Defence Offset Policy", *Strategic Analysis*, Vol. 33, No. 2, March 2009, pp.242–253.
4. Maj Gen (Retd) Bhupinder Yadav, *Indian Defence Offset: A Guide, for Confederation of Indian Industry.*
5. Ministry of Defence, Government of India, *Annual Report 2008-09*
6. Ministry of Defence, Government of India, *Annual Report 2009-10*
7. Ministry of Defence, Government of India, *Defence Procurement Procedure: Capital Procurement 2008.*
8. Ministry of Defence, Government of India, *Defence Procurement Procedure: Capital Procurement 2006.*
9. Ministry of Defence, Government of India, *Defence Procurement Procedure: Capital Procurement 2005.*
10. Ministry of Defence, Government of India, *Defence Procurement Procedure: Capital Procurement 2002.*
11. Ministry of Defence, Government of India, *Defence Services Estimates* (various years)
12. Ministry of Finance, Government of India, *Economic Survey 2009-10.*
13. Standing Committee on Defence (2005-06), Ministry of Defence, 14th Lok Sabha, *Procurement Policy and Procedure.*
14. Thirteenth Finance Commission, 2010-2015, Volume I Report, December 2009.
15. U.S. Department of Commerce, Bureau of Industry and Security, *Offsets in Defence Trade*, 12th Report to Congress.

NOTES

NOTES